A Singular Book of Great Esteem

Life with the I Ching

A Singular Book of Great Esteem

Life with the I Ching

Glenn Martin

G.P. Martin Publishing

Published 2025 by G.P. Martin Publishing

Website: www.glennmartin.com.au

Contact: info@glennmartin.com.au

Book layout and cover design by the author

Typeset in Sitka 11 pt

Printed by Lulu.com

Cover design by the author. Front cover image is Fu Hsi, the Yellow Emperor (~2900 BC) who is said to have devised the eight trigrams on which the I Ching is based.

ISBN: 978 0 6459543 5 7 (pbk.)

NATIONAL LIBRARY OF AUSTRALIA

A catalogue record for this book is available from the National Library of Australia

Man expends his energy upon the outer world without let or hindrance. In the midst of this extraversion, the "continent of the spirit" recedes on the horizon. Does it still exist? The new edition of this book is an affirmative answer. It reminds us that man never really loses his vision of the "continent of the spirit" and that the conquest of "inner space", the understanding of the psyche, will remain the ultimate human goal.

Cary Baynes, Translator's note to the new, revised edition of *The Secret of the Golden Flower* by Richard Wilhelm, 1962.

Continue to rectify things; this is the way of heaven.

(19: Approach; John Blofeld)

Contents

Preface

I had embarked, tentatively, on a project to write about the I Ching. Tentatively, because there are enough good books on the I Ching, and one should not be presumptuous. I was beginning to think I had an approach that was worth exploring when I had an episode, a severe headache that lasted all day, that was subsequently interpreted by the medical professionals as a stroke.

For a couple of weeks I was waylaid, functional enough for ordinary living, but unable to proceed smoothly with the project. I had some periods of lucidity when I wrote some more, but the path was, I have to say, muddled. I had to face the question of what had happened, and why. At the same time, I had to consider whether these questions were related to the project itself.

This, of course, is the very territory of the I Ching. I maintained my practice of conversing with the I Ching daily, and boldened myself to ask it direct questions. Accordingly, over the next few weeks, the project took shape, and my resolve clarified. What resolve?

I resolved to trust in the path as it presents itself. It may not sound like much, but perhaps it is enough. Perhaps it is everything. I trust that you will enjoy the book.

Glenn Martin, Cherrybrook

January 2025

0 The Beginning

I have used the I Ching for around fifty years. I have accumulated a good collection of books on the subject. I think most people who use the I Ching have just one book or a few books that they use regularly. I had the one book for over twenty years: Richard Wilhelm's translation, which was completed in German in 1923, and then translated into English in 1950 by (Ms) Cary Baynes.

This book became a bestseller, a cult classic, if you will. It crept through the counterculture in the 1960s. Lots of people said they were familiar with it. Lots of people said they consulted it and heeded its advice. It cropped up in unexpected places: Tom Hanks mentioned it as a source of wisdom in the movie "You've Got Mail" (noting that his other source of wisdom was "The Godfather").

Someone gave a copy of the I Ching to me, at that time in my early twenties when I was first poking my head outside of Christianity. It was exotic. I was unfamiliar with Chinese philosophy, or with where the I Ching sat in Chinese culture, either ancient or modern. I learned that its past went back nearly 5,000 years, so it was older than all the treasures of world literature: Beowulf, Old Testament scriptures, the Code of Hammurabi, stories from ancient Egypt, ancient Greece, ancient Rome, ancient India.

There was only one other I Ching book that I knew about: James Legge's translation from 1882. I had a copy of it but I didn't use it much. I was familiar with Wilhelm's book and that was that. Things began to change when I went into a shop that sold spiritual books and found a different translation: Alfred Huang's book, *The Complete I Ching*. Huang had had a different past to Wilhelm. He was Chinese, and he had learned the I Ching as a young man during the early days of Communist China. He had learned it in secret, in Shanghai, as it had already been denounced as one of the old superstitions that should be discarded.

Huang was eventually arrested, and he spent around twenty years in a re-education camp. He was skin and bone when he was finally released. He went to America after this, and eventually he decided to write a book on the I Ching: a new translation. For him it was a matter of doing that or seeing his knowledge die out.

I retained my respect for Richard Wilhelm, but I was most interested in what I might learn from Alfred Huang. I was very much aware of the fact that Wilhelm had studied in the company of a Chinese teacher for twenty years, so I wasn't about to reject what I had learned from him. But I did not treat my knowledge as final or fixed; it was more about broadening and enriching my point of view.

There was also the more general idea that Wilhelm had done his work in the Beijing of the early 1900s as a Westerner, and Huang was Chinese and from a different area of China. Accordingly, I bought Huang's book and immersed myself in it happily for a couple of years.

There were particular aspects where Huang brought enrichment, such as his treatment of the ideographs (Chinese script for the hexagram names). He also included stories from the time of King Wen and his son, the Duke of Chou (or Zhou, who played a major part in the development of the I Ching that we know, around 1,100 BC).

After the advent of the internet, and the rise of online bookshops, there was a flowering of my I Ching collection. I acquired books from around the world. Many of them were recent, in line with the increase in studies of the I Ching around the world, along with studies in languages and new methods of research. New archaeological finds had also occurred, so understanding should have improved generally.

There were numerous Chinese masters living in the U.S., such as Tai Chi practitioners. There were Chinese scholars living in Asia. There were Western scholars who had immersed themselves in the language and culture of China. There were many people who had encountered the I Ching and who had immersed themselves in it and developed a particular perspective on it: psychology, mythology, spiritual development, decision-making.

It is surprising, and it seems strange, that the I Ching can be used today as a living tool, given its extraordinary age and its origin in a far distant culture. Yet Wilhelm took it seriously. Carl Jung, the Swiss psychotherapist who wrote the Foreword for Wilhelm's version of the I Ching, took it seriously. Alfred Huang took it seriously. The I Ching is in a class of its own. It maintains its relevance. It challenges you to examine the circumstances of your life in an all-embracing context, and to see it in terms of morality and purpose.

1 A more recent beginning

It started in a bookshop. I asked if they had any books about the I Ching. I was directed to a particular section of the shop, where I found just one book. It happened to be the first publication on the I Ching that I had acquired about fifty years ago: Richard Wilhem's *I Ching or Book of Changes*, translated from German into English by Cary Baynes and first published by Bollingen (at Princeton University in the U.S.) in 1950. (Prior to this, the version in German was completed in 1923.)

I know that's too much information, but this book was the bedrock for my understanding of the I Ching, and the English version was released in the year I was born. And I know, these days coincidences are scorned, as if we live in the era of science where everything has to be proven, but so be it. So be it.

The shock about the single copy of the I Ching in the bookshop was that, when I opened it up, it was a facsimile copy. This means that the text is all muddy, as if a photocopy has been photocopied again and again on a less-than-perfect machine. The book is 740 pages of fine text, and it doesn't wear well after such treatment.

Let me say the circumstances under which I will tolerate facsimile editions, and I have an example. I had a book which I had found in a library in a distant town in Queensland. It was a most unexpected find. I borrowed it and read it avidly, as they say, and it changed my way of looking at some aspects of life, as a good book should. I bought it from the library. Then I lent it to somebody, and as is common, I didn't get it back, and as is also common, I couldn't remember whom I had lent it to.

Nevertheless. I still wanted to have the book, so I found it online and ordered it. When it came (from England, where the book was originally published), I discovered it was a facsimile copy, and yes, I found the text somewhat muddy. But I had the book, for which I was both delighted and grateful! The key factor is this: it would never have been a best seller. It was written by an Anglican nun in England and it was probably bought and read by a rather small group of people. It was not something I ever expected to find, and I considered the reprinting to be a kindness.

On the contrary, Richard Wilhelm's book on the I Ching was bought by millions of people. It was published in Britain and the United States, and was reprinted multiple times. It's not as if the files for the book had been lost, or the publisher had disappeared.

So, I was saddened by the new book in the bookshop, as well as by the fact that it was the only book on the subject they had. On the way home on the train, I thought about why this might be. Was the single book a sop to the possibility of a solitary person being interested in the book? As if it had been a trend that had dwindled and died?

If it sold, perhaps it would be an indication of a modest revival, and perhaps the next time ordering was done, they would order three copies of the book, or branch out and buy a different book on the I

Ching (although all the staff were young, and one suspects that there was no knowledge of the I Ching among them). And perhaps the book had been on the shelves for a long time, and it had been subject to banishment more than once, but someone decided, each time, that it was the only book on that subject, and we are supposed to be a comprehensive bookshop, aren't we? We are supposed to have "everything".

In my library, my home library, I have 110 metres of shelf space for books, and there is not much of that space that is spare. Of the 110 metres, nearly three metres is devoted to books about the I Ching and the *Tao Te Ching*. It is a collection that has grown from one and then two books to, well, three metres. Let us say, my collection is probably quite comprehensive.

Then I think, if you knew nothing about the I Ching, perhaps Wilhelm's book would seem daunting. My start was when I was given the book in my early twenties. It was given to me by someone (whom I no longer know). I have heard it said that there are some books you should get involved with only if they are given to you, rather than you buying it.

I am slightly suspicious of statements like this; they seem simply superstitious. If I had had the idea that I wanted to find out about the I Ching, I probably would have bought it, guilt-free. It just didn't happen that way, although perhaps the fact that it was given to me does mean something significant.

I followed the instructions in the book to get started. You need three coins (preferably Chinese, with a square hole in the middle), and you have to shake them up in your cupped hands and then throw them down. Meanwhile, you are concentrating on a question in your mind, a question on which you would like some guidance. According to which sides of the coins are face up after this manoeuvre, there is a line that you draw. You do this six times. This gives you a hexagram (sometimes two hexagrams), and a reading in the book. (See Appendix 1: Moving Lines.)

Once you open the book, you are faced with sixty-four readings, which are based on paired combinations of any of eight images: Heaven, Thunder, Water, Mountain, Earth, Wind, Fire, and Lake. It would be understandable if one felt lost. How could this be helpful, or offer any kind of guidance?

When I first started, I thought: you have be willing to be a beginner. This is a very comprehensive system of thought, and it has been around in its current form for about three thousand years, aside from the fact that its roots lie another two thousand years further into the past. Being a beginner means you will come up against things that are opaque, and you have to be willing for understanding to come gradually, with continued practice.

I also thought that many people today would not have the patience for this. They would say, "Give me the answer now!" But our wiser selves know that this is called impatience, and impatience is not usually rewarded. What might one learn over time? Could it be worthwhile? Could it be illuminating?

Now, I have used this book for decades, in many different circumstances: problems at work, problems with politics at work, problems with relationships, problems with money, or choice of a place to live. One lesson was, it didn't always tell me what I wanted to hear. One time I had been the manager of an organisation for several years when an atmosphere of opposition began to build in the management committee. This went on for months. There were some unsavoury people pushing their weight around, and their lies (told with malice) were poisoning the situation.

Things were shifting towards a crisis. The I Ching told me "Peace" (11), which is where Heaven and Earth are in a sublime, positive relationship with one another. The next day I got sacked. At first I was dumbfounded. But, as the situation unfolded, I began to see that the sacking was the best way for the situation to end. I wasn't going to win: the politics were stacked against me, and how do you fight lies, anyway? Especially when the bulk of people watching are passive, and are ready to accept the loudest voice in the room. We are suckers for people who have unabashed confidence.

The only thing left to find was peace, and the only way I was going to find peace was to be thrust out of that situation. By being sacked, I was being saved. A hard lesson. And yes, I could have handled things differently, and in future situations I did (more strategy, less crude defiance), but the lesson was learned here, through the I Ching.

That's to step a long way ahead. Are there some I Ching books I would recommend to the bookshop? Yes, I would have some recommendations. That may become clear. On the other hand, I would have reservations about making recommendations. We all travel our own path.

It is unbelievable, perhaps, that I relied on Wilhelm's book for thirty years before I found another. But this was not a bad thing. I got to know Wilhelm's way of thinking very well. He was a Protestant German minister who went to China as a missionary in the 1890s, but he ended up spending most of his time there learning the I Ching from an old Chinese master. From the book you understand that the conversations he had with this master must have been very deep and satisfying. (His master's name was Lao Nai-Hsuan.)

2 Finding a new I Ching

For a long time, I had never really wondered about whether there were other books on the I Ching. Then, one day I was in a bookshop on the Central Coast (north of Sydney), which had an agglomeration of New Age books and artefacts, and I saw such a book. So, the idea dawned on me that there were other books on the I Ching. Diving in at once, I bought the book. It was Alfred Huang's *The Complete I Ching* (mentioned above). He was Chinese, which I thought made a lot of sense: there had to be someone Chinese who knew about the I Ching, despite Chairman Mao and his ruthless modernisation program. Everything old was spurned as superstition; the future was going to be indomitably materialistic.

There was no room in Chinese Communism for "ancient Chinese wisdom" which was described in Wilhelm's book as mysterious and sacred. For Wilhelm, it was unquestionably one of the most important books in the world's literature. Alfred Huang's story was, appropriately, a product of the Maoist modernisation blunderbuss. When young, Huang had studied with Taoist masters, and had become a Professor of Taoist Philosophy.

Alfred Huang was from a family that had a tradition in the Taoist practice of Tai Chi Chuan. It was in 1966 that he became a casualty of the Cultural Revolution. He was imprisoned and sentenced to death. Although reprieved, he spent another thirteen years in prison, and when he was finally released he weighed only thirty-six kilograms. He emigrated to the United States, and through teaching healing and teaching the I Ching, he was inspired to produce a translation of the I Ching.

Alfred Huang's translation was a great insight for me. Here was a very different perspective to that of Wilhelm, but consistent with it. It wasn't as if they were at odds with each other. I think if they had met, they would have stood their own ground, but yet held great respect for the other. In introducing each hexagram, Huang

9

compares his name for it with the names used by Wilhelm and one other person, John Blofeld (we may get to him in due course).

Say, for 46, Sheng, Huang calls it "Growing Upward", then says "Wilhelm translates Sheng as Pushing Upward and Blofeld as Ascending, Promotion". Then Huang gives his reasons for choosing the name he did. I'm sure the reason Huang refers to Wilhelm and Blofeld is because they were both already so well-known with Western audiences, but I also think there is respect, as if to say, "You came from the West to this most different culture, and yet you learned well."

Huang also had other points of difference. There is an ideograph for each hexagram, and I hadn't taken much notice of them before. Huang drew the ideographs in big, chunky brush strokes, where you could see the different components of them clearly. In so doing, he opened them up so that they became another language for me, and my appreciation of the I Ching increased.

For example, two brush strokes represent a person, and it is done the same way in all the hexagrams where it occurs. That shape that looks like a rectangle with the bottom missing, and a short line in the centre at the top, represents a house with a chimney. The shape that looks like a man with his arms and legs stretched out wide stands for a great man. The sun and the moon are also represented in a certain way.

Each hexagram is made up of two trigrams, so the meaning is made up by how the two trigrams relate to each other. For example, Sheng (46) is made up of Wood below Earth, so you can see how the meaning is in the image of a plant "growing upward".

So, what happens if Wood is above Earth? You get 20, Guan; in English, Watching. The wood above the earth is a tower, from which one watches, and the ideograph features eyes: a bird's eye, and a human eye. One also watches oneself; introspection is the first step in self-development.

46: Growing Upwards:
Sheng

20: Watching: Guan

I spent many months absorbing Alfred Huang's perspective. He also extended the stories of the I Ching. The time around 1,100 BC was a pivotal time in Chinese history, as the Shang dynasty was under strain. It was at this time that King Wen and the Duke of Zhou (his son) put together the I Ching in its current form.

King Wen had been a vassal king to the Shang emperor, who was a tyrant: cruel, selfish and indulgent, an oppressor. In time, King Wen rallied support to overthrow the emperor, but for a time he was imprisoned. While in prison, he worked on the development of the I Ching as a system of sixty-four hexagrams made up of the pairings of all the combinations of the eight trigrams, and he produced the corresponding commentary for each hexagram.

The Duke of Zhou continued the work on the commentary after his father's death until it was completed. This is what become the preeminent source of wisdom in China for almost the next three thousand years. When Wilhelm and a few other Europeans explored the I Ching in the nineteenth and early twentieth centuries, they took something that was being strangled in its homeland and offered it to the world.

It seems appropriate that Alfred Huang experienced prison just as King Wen did, and in both cases they served the purposes of the I Ching, the great vehicle of wisdom. Richard Wilhelm's work on the translation of the I Ching was interrupted by the Chinese revolution of 1911, and then again by the first World War, when the Japanese besieged Peking (Beijing).

Wilhem observes that while he worked on the I Ching in the besieged city, the commander of the besieging Japanese troops was studying the works of the Chinese scholar Mencius at night. (I don't know how he knew this, but we have to accept that, afterwards, many things become known.)

3 The I Ching for today

How can we refer to the I Ching as "the great vehicle of wisdom"? Isn't that slightly ridiculous in our scientifically enlightened times? When I consider the single, impaired copy of the I Ching in the central-city bookshop, I wonder. Is it an irrelevance now? Is my attention to the I Ching an irrelevance? Was Chairman Mao right? The superstitious villagers needed to be woken up, or they would never progress?

This smacks of simplistic judgement. The truth is, there was probably a percentage of truth in Chairman Mao's judgements, but changes in societies are seldom achieved with nuance. And there is also the fact that people come to enjoy destroying things, and people. Just as the Shang emperor did, just as Hitler did.

Or, is it that we live in divided times, accelerated by the internet, and people just join fiefdoms where people agree with each other? So, perhaps there is a fiefdom where the I Ching is lauded, and other fiefdoms where it is derided. And if so, there is no need to consider what people in the other fiefdoms think. We just need to find the fiefdom where the other people agree with what we think.

I am not in favour of this perspective. How does one learn to think for oneself unless one can stand apart at times? The I Ching says "the wise person can stand alone without regret when necessary". A book, one must remember, is dormant. Books await our response. As

Stefan Zweig (Austrian writer, 1881-1942) said: "The books are there, waiting and silent. They neither urge, nor press their claims."

Conversely, I could say the wisdom is not in the book; one must appropriate the wisdom. Nevertheless, we would all recognise that in many books, the soil is indeed shallow. Not much of lasting value will ensue from the time you spend with them.

On the other hand, a book can change the way you see things. And some books, you may spend a lot of time with them. It is a question of whether they open your mind or shut it down. In life there are ruts, and there may be comfort in them. One can choose to follow in a rut, and even call it wisdom or truth. But in the end, you have to make that judgement for yourself. It's easier to think that another person is deluded than to have this thought about yourself.

Suppose you accept that the I Ching might be a useful book to spend time with. How are you going to test that? (I offer no answer, but I ask, how are you going to test that?)

Next: spending time with the I Ching will take time, especially when you read it the way that is recommended. As modern, economically educated people, we understand the concept of opportunity cost. The time you spend on one thing is time taken away from something else you could be doing. That is the terror of modern life. All that time I spent at the beach, I could have been working. Or, all that time I spent working, I could have been at the beach. Every way, you suffer from missing out on something.

And if the I Ching takes a lot of time, the opportunity cost is high. In times to come, economists may be sorry for poisoning life in this way. No wonder modern sages advocate that we learn to "be here now". The I Ching will take time. Call it time spent being here now.

Next: luck. Luck is a prominent concept in Chinese thought. A good life has the intention to be upright, but to this is added discipline, and…. luck. What does this mean? It applies in the way we read the I Ching. Normally, one would begin at the beginning and continue until one has reached the end. But we do not do this. We sit, throw the I Ching coins, and look up the one or two hexagrams to which it takes us. There are sixty-four, so we could be looking in any one or two places within the covers of the book.

Oh yes, I recommend that you read the introduction first, whatever version you have chosen. One needs context.

This leads to the question of when you throw the I Ching. It depends on what your purpose is. Popularly, the I Ching is a fortune-teller. You use it when you have a question about some situation you are involved in, and you want some guidance. So then, you will use the I Ching when you face such a question. Then, it depends on whether you just use it when you are thinking about changing jobs, or whether you want to ask it everyday questions like, should I go out with this person?

The instructions for the use of the I Ching tell you to hold the question in your mind as you throw the coins.

Yet, there is another way to use the I Ching. It is not called a book of wisdom for nothing. Suppose you sit down with the I Ching, and you open yourself to everything that is in your life at the moment. Then, you know that the I Ching knows everything about you anyway, and you throw the coins. When you get the hexagram, or hexagrams, and read what they have to say, you will be able to see which issues it is commenting on, even if you didn't want to think about them.

"Reading the book" in this way could take a long time, even years, because it depends on luck. It took me a long time before I felt that I had probably read all of Wilhelm's book. There is one commentary (by Richard Rudd) that I have been reading, in a variation of this method, for nearly five years. I only read this book when I receive a hexagram with no moving lines.

Using this rule, there are only two of the sixty-four hexagrams that I have not received at all yet (hexagrams with no moving lines), and on the other hand there is one hexagram I have thrown eleven times, and another, nine times. There are twelve hexagrams that I have thrown just once or twice.

In writing here about the I Ching, I am going to reveal things as I go. I guess that readers are curious about things I allude to. What are the two hexagrams I have thrown a lot of times?

Lu (10), which is Conduct, I have thrown eleven times. This leads us to the next point: what does it mean if you throw a particular hexagram a lot? In this case, does it mean I am very regularly guilty of misconduct? I don't think that, but it does tell me I need to keep my focus on this aspect of living. There are two things in life: action, and the regulation of actions, that is, ethics. Both are necessary if one is to live a worthwhile life.

Beyond this, what do I have to say about 10: Conduct? In my three metres of I Ching books, I have about ten that I use regularly. This gives me a rich perspective on the hexagram. The writers highlight different aspects of it. We have to remember that the I Ching is not a legal text to be interpreted as if we were lawyers. The line of discrimination is not about what is a right view and what is wrong. It would be closer to say the I Ching, in its various versions, is a painting or a poem that we are trying to interpret.

Wilhelm says of this hexagram: "the superior man (person) discriminates between high and low, and thereby fortifies the thinking of the people." But the hexagram contains the idea of treading as well, and here, one treads upon the tail of a tiger, but it does not bite. There will be progress and success. The way will be prosperous and smooth. Huang says, fulfil your duty. Sometimes, in doing so, the weak must tread upon the powerful. If one treads with firm steps, and remains upright, one may be successful. He points at the combination of tact and clarity that is needed.

Richard Rudd says that in each hexagram, there are three things: there is a shadow side, a gift, and a place of bliss (he uses the Sanskrit word, siddhi). For Conduct, he says the shadow side is selfishness, or self-obsession. But if one endeavours to move beyond this, cultivating upright conduct, one discovers that it is a natural, innocent (but not naïve) state. This is the innocence that causes the tiger to not bite the person. In fact, the person draws in something of the strength of the tiger. The siddhi for this hexagram is simply "Being". It is an extension of innocence, or the fulness of innocence.

Huang actually calls this hexagram Fulfilment, meaning, the fulfilment of one's duty. The ideograph is a picture of a person walking in shoes.

What of the other hexagram I have thrown multiple times? It is 37: Family: Jia Ren. One can ask the same question: why? Is it because of my own defectiveness in this department? Is it because of the importance of families in my life, or in the overall functioning of society? Or is it because the question of roles within families is vexed in our current society, and it needs a lot of thinking?

I have taken the observations of this hexagram as a commentary on my own experiences with family, both good and bad. Secondly, I have taken the hexagram as an observation on my explorations of my family history. And thirdly, I have engaged with my various books on the I Ching for what they have to say about the changing climate for families today, and the implications of changes in gender roles. Do they recognise them, ignore them or reject them?

We know there are religious families that take on the male and female roles just as they were expounded more than a thousand years ago and apply them strictly, ignoring all social changes that have occurred since then. The male is the boss and the female is silent and subservient. It is obvious that there is little inherent wisdom in this. Is there a way of understanding what is said in the I Ching that makes sense today?

For a start, it is not so simple. Wilhelm's version says, "the women obtain the proper place within, the men obtain the proper place without". This seems to say that women should direct matters within the household, while men should direct matters in the outside world. Regardless, we have to accept that women today are often working outside the house, and this demands a rethink of the division of roles within the house.

In discussing the family, Wilhelm focuses on roles and the relationships between them. We see this differently if we are considering principles rather than trying to impose strict rules. Wilhelm says each person should be able to find their appropriate expression in the family. He also says there must be leadership in the family; it is not an anarchy. And the leadership must come from the parents. Then he says that the foundation of the family is the relationship between the husband and the wife.

Beyond this we have to step deftly among the social practices of the times when the texts were written. In Wilhelm's case, it was the early twentieth century in Europe and China. For Huang it was the times he lived through in China when the society was disintegrating and Communist culture came to be the dominant force, viewed through the lens of ancient China. What is principle, and what is "local" practice?

Also, there is the Confucian perspective. Huang refers to Confucius, who said the government of a state depends on the regulation of the family. When people respect each other within the family, in an understanding of their place within the structure, the state will be at peace. If there is love between husband and wife, between brothers and sisters, and between parents and children, there will be peace in the country.

It is easy to make utopian statements, and what Confucius said could be considered to be trite, but I think it is worthwhile to dig for principles in a changing world. Modern society has made strides: we promote the principle of equality, for example, but we quickly reduce it to rigid, and often arbitrary, expectations. In the context of the I

Ching, the lesson I learned is that it is a whole, and nothing can be understood outside of the entire context.

One example: I said above that there must be leadership in the family, and it must come from the parents (both of them). In order to understand what leadership is, one learns from other hexagrams. And that understanding leads us also, frequently, to the *Tao Te Ching*. This brief text was written by Lao Tzu around 500 BC, and it is accepted by I Ching commentators as the most sublime expression of truths in the I Ching.

We are exposed in our society to leadership as an act of dominance and force, sometimes, even, an act of guile. This style of leadership is even promoted, as if these were virtues. The Tao says, "Whenever you advise a ruler in the way of Tao, counsel him not to use force to conquer the universe, for this would only cause resistance." The Tao says, "A violent man will die a violent death."

Thus, when thinking of leadership in the family, one must think of the Tao.

4 Regular consultation

After I discovered Alfred Huang, things went quietly for a while. I was content with my two books, and the contrasts in their two perspectives. I was consulting the I Ching regularly. I was still erratic, in the sense that I wrote notes on scraps of paper and in random notepads, never thinking about keeping those notes as a record of my perusing and study.

Looking back, the shift was gradual. Firstly, I might have kept notes for a week, or a month or two, then dropped it. Then I would start another book or notepad and do the same. Now that I have compiled all the notebooks together, many of them have just the first few pages written in. And it wasn't until much later that I actually began to write notes, rather than just draw the hexagrams.

Currently (because one never says "forever"), I keep notes in books systematically. I do it every day. I write notes from whichever commentary I am consulting, generally about one A4 page long. The book is always a student notebook, about 100 pages long, so it will generally extend over about three months.

There are different ways to describe what I am doing. One version is, I am simply practising writing. From this perspective, I am getting better. Once was a time when I could hardly read my own writing if I was looking back more than a month ago. Now it looks quite, well, practised. Not as good as typed words, but it is nevertheless easily read.

You could also say that one better remembers material that one has written, rather than simply read (or listened to). I'm not sure if this truth is even remembered today, when people are often merely skimming words on a screen and, at most, highlighting phrases with the computer's highlighter or, if on paper, using a highlighter pen. The damning criticism of my practice is that I am "old-fashioned".

I do not deny that I was fashioned in another era. (And yet, I am comfortably typing on a computer.)

There is something else: as I am writing, I am in fact summarising, and of necessity, rephrasing what I am reading. And I will happen upon insights in this way. What I think I am getting better at is understanding ideas. I also find that I am remembering things that I read a while ago in another book of commentary, and that gets integrated into today's notes as well.

Now I have to talk about one's state of mind. My practice occurs in the morning. My commiserations to people who have a clock-job, that is, one that demands you be available at a certain time each morning, so your time is not your own. I have served my time, and now nobody misses me if I am not at a particular place at nine o'clock each morning.

But, I also think we should do what we can to create our own structure of the day or the week, the aim being to have a space for a practice which is not impinged upon. This can be different for each person. Adhere to the principle; it is not a matter of sticking to fixed rules invented by someone else, no matter how allegedly holy or authoritative.

This is the pre-condition to one's state of mind. So, when I am writing my notes, I am not trying to be clever. In our society, "mind" means being clever. I grew up with Western mind: I know about being clever. So, if not clever, what? Some of the I Ching commentators say that instead of clever-mind, we need to think of heart-mind, or heart-and-mind as being one unified entity. One thinks with the heart, and the mind is the servant of the heart. So, one is seeking the heart's truth.

Lest this be thought of disparagingly as Eastern twaddle, or "going soft", or airy-fairy, or New-Agey – this litany of scorn is forever growing – let me note that this topic is being addressed by scientifically minded people in the West. For example, Iain McGilchrist (2019): *The Master and His Emissary: The Divided Brain and the Making of the Western World.*

I stop a long way short of saying I am discovering "truth". That would be yet another conceit to fall into. I like the word "insight", because it implies that one is seeing further into something. There is no absolutism in it; one can keep looking more deeply, and one's understanding can be extended and enriched. And it leaves one still in the field, still alert for the onset of delusion.

I skipped over a step: which commentary am I reading? But, we can't get to that just yet. What is the difference between the I Ching and commentary on the I Ching? Is it like the Bible, namely, there are scholars in search of the correct, or original, version of the text? And then some other scholars write commentary about it?

The same problems of time apply, except that for the I Ching, the timespan is much longer. Wilhelm was studying with an old I Ching scholar, who consulted what was the source for him in Beijing in the early twentieth century, adding: this was also an oral tradition, passed on for generations from teacher to student. When Wilhelm's translation of the I Ching was published, it became the standard for about fifty years. Note, it was a translation.

What was exciting for me in discovering Alfred Huang was that he came from a different time, place and perspective, so he would throw a different light upon the I Ching. In his Introduction, Huang does refer to Wilhelm. Huang's learning in the I Ching came when he was a young adult, in Shanghai, and it came at a time when Mao Tse Tung, after his accession to power, was striving to conquer the hearts and minds of the Chinese people for Communism. In the early 1960s, the I Ching had already been denounced as feudalistic and superstitious. It was banned from being sold.

Alfred Huang was part of a small circle of men who learned the I Ching in secret from an old master who wanted to pass it on before knowledge of it died. The teacher, Master Yin, had himself learned the I Ching from his own master. They also held the view that the I Ching had to be transmitted orally, or it would be misunderstood.

Unfortunately, we don't all have the luxury of a private teacher, and especially in the situation that Huang was in – their meetings had to be held in secret, for fear of arrest by the police – it becomes too hard to say that the only way you can learn it is in person.

Besides that, I do love the capacity of books to extend knowledge far beyond what is possible personally. Yes, there is the possibility of misunderstandings but, as I say: nevertheless!

Also, it is essential that study is individual rather than just participating in group study under a teacher. Huang himself quotes a saying of Confucius: "If some years were added to my life, I would dedicate fifty years to the study of the Book of I, and then I might come to be without fault." This was a statement Confucius made when he was seventy.

The "Book of I" is the Book of Changes. Ching means "the great classic", and "I" means changes. The underpinning perspective of the I Ching is that everything in life is in continuous change, because it is subject to the ongoing dynamic between yin and yang. Yin and yang are constantly seeking to find balance and harmony. As the Zen saying goes: one never steps into the same river twice.

Why is Confucius quoted? It is because Confucius produced commentaries on the I Ching; they are known as the Ten Wings. The Ten Wings are said to make the words of the I Ching fly. I have read books on the I Ching by Western authors who scorn the words of Confucius, and who maintain that his work is not part of the I Ching. Wilhelm is not one of those; nor is Huang.

To me, the Ten Wings are needed. They help us to understand what is being said in the I Ching. I also think the work of faithful modern authors is needed, if they help us to recognise the import of context. For example, hexagram 48 is called The Well. To understand what this hexagram is saying, one must have some understanding of the place of the well in ancient village life. Huang says, "The site of a village may be moved, but not the well."

Note that Wilhelm renders the text as: "The town may be changed, but the well cannot be changed." It would be wrong to give the impression that Huang and Wilhelm are far apart; mostly they are not. I have respect for Wilhelm's teacher, Lao Nai-Hsuan, as well as Huang's teacher, Master Yin.

There is another stream of thought as well, about whether Confucius actually wrote all the Ten Wings, or whether parts of the commentary were written after he died. There is even the idea that some parts were written before the time of Confucius, that is, they were picked up for the commentary from existing writings. And, of course, there is an argument that Confucius never existed, that the commentary is the product of an on-flowing stream of scholars who constituted a school of thought. And to the contrary, there is the view that the idea of famous people never having existed is merely a temporary scholastic fad.

I am of the view that numerous individuals who belong to a community which is devoted to a school of thought may contribute to the writings which it produces. This may be of interest, but it does not need to undermine the writings. Presumably the writings were issued with the agreement of the community.

5 Translating the I Ching

When Richard Wilhelm was working on his translation of the I Ching, the material he worked with belonged to the scholarly tradition: texts that had been handed down through many masters. There were issues enough in translating the Chinese into German and then into English. Cary Baynes, who did the translation from German into English, commented that the rendition Wilhelm made of the Chinese was sometimes different from the translation made by James Legge, who had done a translation of the I Ching in 1882. But finding a way to render the Chinese text in *any* other language was demanding.

Both Wilhelm and Legge spent over twenty years on their translations. There were (and are) many difficulties in translating the Chinese text. For many of the Chinese terms, there is no exact equivalent in English, or German. Therefore, translation must be accompanied by interpretation, and sometimes it is difficult to disentangle one from the other. Moreover, many Chinese characters have multiple meanings. And often, the ideas are profound philosophical concepts.

Wilhelm's book has a Foreword by Carl Jung. Jung says, "The I Ching does not offer itself with proofs and results; it does not vaunt itself, nor is it easy to approach. Like a part of nature, it waits until it is discovered. It offers neither facts nor power, but for lovers of self-knowledge, of wisdom – if there be such – it seems to be the right book. To one person its spirit appears as clear as day; to another, shadowy as twilight; to a third, dark as night. He who is not pleased by it does not have to use it, and he who is against it is not obliged to find it true."

Jung had deep respect for Wilhelm. After Wilhelm's death in 1930, he gave an address at a memorial for him in Munich. He said that his translation of the I Ching was not done as a learned outsider, but as a pupil of a Chinese master, and as one who had a lived experience of the I Ching. He said Wilhelm had transmitted to us "the living germ of the Chinese spirit, capable of working an essential change in our view of life".

Jung credited Wilhelm with having fulfilled the extraordinarily important cultural task of bringing the I Ching to the West. Around one hundred years later, this still feels true to me.

To return to the same question: what are the original sources of the I Ching?, we should note comments made by Hellmut Wilhelm, Richard Wilhelms's son, that after his father had completed his work, scholars of the twentieth century discovered and examined very old materials: inscriptions on oracle bones, which added to the understanding of parts of the I Ching. There were also new studies being done in analysing the language and structure of the book. It is now generally accepted that the book assumed its current form around a hundred years prior to the life of Confucius, that is, several hundred years after the time of King Wen and the Duke of Zhou.

Hellmut Wilhelm describes the book as "a unique manifestation of the human mind". Cary Baynes (Wilhelm's translator) notes that it is extremely important that China's recorded history is around three thousand years long, continuously, so that the text was not subject to upheavals and periods of obscurity.

Other scholars have contributed different perspectives on the book. Stephen Karcher focuses on myth, divination, depth psychology and religious practices. His books on the I Ching apply these perspectives to the text. He considers various societies and their beliefs and practices at the time when the book was created. He describes his version of the book (he wrote several, but the primary one is *Total I Ching: Myths for Change*) as poetic rather than an historical translation, although it is based on extensive scholarly studies. He is interested in the I Ching as a tool for self-development, and he is interested in the various aspects and layers of the person, exploring myths and symbols to do so.

Karcher says that since the Wilhelm-Baynes edition of the I Ching in 1950, the concepts in the I Ching have become part of Western imagination and spirituality, although an underground part.

Hua-Ching Ni, another teacher of the I Ching in modern times, was born in China in 1925, into a family with a long tradition of healing and spirituality. He moved to the United States in 1976. He has written over forty books. His major work on the I Ching is called *The Book of Changes and the Unchanging Truth*. It discusses the principles that underlie the I Ching as a foundation for living naturally and developing spiritually.

What does he say to the new reader? He says that in this modern age, we are benefitting from technological advances, but we are also facing the fearsome threat of potential destruction. Nothing remains untouched by our scientific explorations, but we have become overwhelmed by our own creations. What is needed is a correct way of thinking that can guide us to safety and prosperity. It will encourage the full development of individual life, as well as the peaceful regulation of families and nations.

When we become confused, we become victims to opportunists, driven by unbridled ambition, who would seize the reins of social leadership, often through insidious actions. What is needed is the discovery of inner light to correctly direct our life's energies.

The I Ching, he says, is the teaching of the Integral Way, deep truth that conveys the Subtle Essence of life. It is not an external authority; nor does it belong to the emotional surface of life; and it is not locked to the level of thought or belief. It provides us with guidance through the trials of life, to find clarity and direction that we do not find in the ordinary converse of modern society.

There are many books on the I Ching that could be described as the coffee table variety: they offer a basic text of the I Ching, invariably based on Wilhelm's version, and they are dressed up in a nice presentation, or they claim to address a particular audience (I Ching for lovers, or managers, or writers). However, they tend to be rudimentary and shallow. The implication is: they are not accurate, and they are unlikely to be really helpful.

How does one know what would be a good place to start? There are many books on the I Ching.... What are the relevant criteria? Accuracy is one criterion. Another is ease of access – can you understand it, that is, the language it uses? Thirdly, does it offer an introduction that allows you to acquire some understanding of the nature of the book?

Being the most recent book is not a credible criterion. Legge's translation from the 1880s is still respected (and found in bookshops). Richard Wilhelm's from 1950 is still regarded with deep respect, and is still the basis for many other "lighter" translations. And in the bookshop where I had the shock of only finding one I Ching book, at least the book was Wilhelm's.

However, the broader perspective is that of John Minford, whose I Ching book is subtitled *The Essential Translation of the Ancient Chinese Oracle and Book of Wisdom*. He says, "I have gradually come to realise (as many others have before me) that there can never be a definitive version of the I Ching in any language. Its 'meaning' is simply too elusive. All interpretations and translations are works in progress. Part of the book's Power is precisely that it has meant so many different things to so many different readers and commentators over the ages, including its translators."

My second experience of looking for the I Ching recently was a visit to another big bookshop in the city, where I found a collection of six books. This time, none of them was Wilhelm's version. It did carry James Legge's translation, plus a couple of "coffee table" editions, and three others which I think are worthy of study: Deng Ming-Dao, Thomas Cleary, and John Minford (as just noted). But I own some others that have rewarded regular study.

It is not as if there is only one "right thing to do". The Way opens into a particular path, and the measure is whether you seek for it to be helpful for self-understanding. The I Ching should not be regarded as a tool to equip you for world domination. Deng Ming-Dao is fond of the phrase "steadfast and upright". Let that be your goal.

6 Consulting the I Ching

It is strange, isn't it, that entering the world of the I Ching is bound to take time and practice before you get the lay of the land, but you can't really approach it by reading the book from front to back? You have to ask it questions, throw the coins (there are alternatives to this; some people use yarrow stalks), read what the hexagram has to say, and think how this applies to your question.

This is to say, the I Ching was originally a tool for divination, telling the future. For many people today, the book is seen in the same way. The questions you ask are about getting the I Ching's perspective on a course of action you are considering. It is not as simple as getting a "yes" or a "no". Suppose you were considering a bold new course of action and you received the hexagram 33: Retreat. That would seem to suggest that the time would be better spent in retreat, not in launching out on a new project.

Again, some people would be scornful about a tool that purports to tell the future, or that offers advice about it. But what the I Ching is offering is another way of thinking. Not everything in life can be apprehended by the scientific, logical mind. Take what Geoffrey Redmond (2017) says: "I was particularly fascinated by divination, not as a means of predicting for myself but as an alternative mode of knowledge, one that many still find of value in their lives. Scientism rejects such as not empirically verifiable, but neither is the beauty of a painting verifiable, despite its enhancing life."

We live in a material reality that we can describe. We have learned to describe its numerous dimensions, and we have learned sets of expectations about each of these dimensions. There is money, family, relationships, home, health. Jobs, all with their characteristics. With respect to each of these dimensions, there is a current reality and an implied direction. There are possibilities; and there is luck, or fate. And who are you in the midst of all this?

We may have realised that we are not completely helpless. We have our own perspective on things, and we are responsible for this; it is not imposed. The most powerful expression of the indomitability of the self in the midst of ugly, oppressive, external reality is that of Viktor Frankl in the Nazi Auschwitz concentration camp. In this worst of imaginable circumstances, he said, "It does not really matter what you expect from life, but rather, what life expects from you."

One may arrive at the I Ching wanting magic, wanting it to tell us we will be rich, a winner, loved, admired – all of this – but the I Ching, instead, is watching you, whispering the words of Viktor Frankl. All those prizes are not kept from us; the field is open. But more than this, the I Ching asks if we can be steadfast and upright, if we can live open-heartedly.

Most of all, the I Ching teaches about change. Life is not static. It is in the nature of humans to want to attain a given level of development and then come to rest, but life is eternally moving: rising, falling, retreating, advancing, breathing in, breathing out. It is not a matter of conquering the processes of life, but of moving in accord with them. One may learn when movement can be effortless; one may know when effort is coming from within one's strength, and know how not to extend ourselves beyond our core.

In the I Ching, there is the concept of the person who has learned how to work constructively with change. The various commentators use different terms for it. Deng Ming-Dao talks of the "noble one". Wilhelm uses the term "superior man", so a comment is necessary about language and gender.

English is constructed with references to male and female. Sometimes, sentences are assuming that males are pre-eminent, and women are not relevant to the matter being discussed. However, it is also true that the word "man" is used to represent the entire species: not just men, but men and women. An example of this usage is in the word "mankind". It makes more sense to accept that this is so rather than trying to overturn the entire history of the language and replace it with clumsy, awkward constructions, or eliminating words from the language altogether.

For example: we can say "humanity" instead of "mankind", but sometimes we prefer to use "mankind", for any number of reasons. Sometimes we can be innovative, such as saying "humankind", but such usages are not always possible, and the essential truth that is being forgotten is that sometimes "man" is used to represent both men and women.

We can accept that gender is a current issue, and that the language is being re-examined. Writers can respond to this in various ways. Some writers alternate the use of male and female. Deng Ming-Dao says the "noble one", but one also has to allow for contexts where "his" or "her" is needed. He alternates their use: "Noble one brightens her own virtue"; "Noble one sees perfection and corrects his own faults"; or without referring to gender: "Noble one bestows wealth to those below".

Apart from "superior man" or "noble one", what other terms are used? Alfred Huang uses "the superior person". Stephen Karcher uses "the Noble One". John Minford uses the term "the true gentleman". In doing so, Minford is evoking the ancient ideal of the gentleman, and he chooses this term instead of the "superior man" or the "great man". The term "sage" crops up occasionally in more than one translation.

Hua-Ching Ni avoids the problem by addressing each judgement to the reader directly: "Go ahead to reach for prosperity, victory and honour". If he needs to refer to a person as the subject, he uses the generic "one", such as "In making progress, one should not worry about gain or loss".

The I Ching is a compendium of sixty-four judgements on situations we may face. It is not a textbook on the qualities of the superior person (or gentleman). One book that I have on the I Ching does contain a list of the qualities of the superior person at the back of the book. The author is Wu Wei, whose book I found in a bookshop in Kuala Lumpur. It lists 117 qualities, such as: "He is humble. He is courteous. He is good-natured. He is calm. He is content within himself. He is aware that the universe is unfolding as it should. He is optimistic. He sets a good example. He turns back immediately having discovered that he has strayed from the path of the superior person."

Wu Wei ends his list with an admonition: "Only through daily renewal of character can you continue at the height of your powers." Richard Wilhelm's expression of this thought is: "The sage learns how best to develop himself so that his influence may endure. He must make himself strong in every way, by consciously casting out all that is inferior and degrading."

The I Ching becomes a world that we enter, and we become someone worthy in that world: "The superior person reflects the glory of Heaven's virtue."

7 Interpreting the readings

Geoffrey Redmond, whose translation of the I Ching is a recent occurrence (2017), says that the nature of the sage is to recognise incipience, to see the shape that things are taking, to be aware of the quality of a given time and thus to be able to act appropriately at all times. The sage knows how things will proceed. And further, the sage is thus able to influence the social order.

Nevertheless, the sage confines him/herself to the current situation. He/she does not deign to transform the world. The socialist economist Yanis Varoufakis (*Technofeudalism*, 2024) recounts the situation when he was in a pub in London and he was challenged by a "Cockney Tory": "If you don't like what we have, what would you replace it with? How would it work?"

Varoufakis was grateful that the pub was too noisy for a serious conversation to be held, because he did not have an answer ready to hand. He recalled Karl Marx sitting in the British Library composing *Das Kapital*, articulating a rational and compelling alternative to voracious capitalism. Varoufakis comments on a critic of his earlier book, who wondered how he could advocate socialism and yet appreciate the benefits of entrepreneurship. The arguments about what is the perfect system can extend interminably.

The sage does not have a perfect system to offer. That would be idealism at its worst. It would be to presume that the whole world would fall in love with this system and embrace it completely and collectively, with full understanding. Beware of utopian dreams. Their advocates tend to precipitate hell.

We know there are moments of elegant, balanced fulfilment where everything forms a shimmering tableau, bringing pleasure to the heart, clarity to the mind, and tranquillity to the soul. It does suggest the possibility of a perfect world. The I Ching ponders this in hexagram 22: Adornment. One commentator (R.L. Wing) says we should use such moments only to refine our immediate environment. It is not the time to make major, long-term decisions.

It is preferable to attend to the contents of the vessel rather focusing on the vessel. There are good people under Communism and there are good people under Capitalism. And this is also true of bad people. It is best for one to concentrate on how to be good rather than to try to imagine, and enforce, the perfect system. The latter path ignores the need for goodness in practice.

The value that Geoffrey Redmond offers is the attempt to take the text of the I Ching back to its origins. He is critical of the fact that commentators have cast layers of interpretation and modernisation over the text since its beginnings. In the case of the I Ching, this has been occurring since its inception before the time of Confucius, who lived from 551 BC to 479 BC. And since the I Ching was a privileged book in the realm of government, many scholars paid attention to it and modified it, in small or significant ways that reflected the contemporary culture.

And yet, there is the statement of John Minford, that it is not simple to accurately ascertain the original text, or the meaning of the text. Redmond accuses Wilhelm of bringing Christian concepts into the Chinese context. For example, hexagram 35 is called Advance by Redmond, while Wilhelm calls it Progress. Redmond says that Wilhelm uses the term "Progress" in the modern Western sense, conflating it with technological improvements in society. It could be noted that this is not a Christian concept; it is a capitalist concept.

Although Redmond might read this into Wilhelm's commentary, there is nothing in Wilhelm's commentary to support the contention. Wilhelm is not talking about the progress of a society. He is talking about a time when a person is enjoying political favour.

Redmond also refers to the beliefs of medieval Christianity: the idea that history is negative, because it is moving away from revelation. But he acknowledges that the belief of early Chinese philosophy was similarly negative: "the time had declined from the ideal society of high antiquity".

There is no doubt that Wilhelm's perspective is influenced by his Christianity: "man's real nature is clouded by contact with earthly things and therefore needs purification", but at this time the sun is rising up above the earth and there is rapid, easy progress.

What do other translators say about this hexagram? Hua-Ching Ni says "the sun is illuminating the earth. It is a time when all things flourish." He calls it Progress. Huang calls it "Proceeding Forward". Deng Ming-Dao says, "Brightness emerging above the earth: Advancing."

The constant is the image: in this hexagram the sun is rising above the earth. The implication is clearly expressed by Hua-Ching Ni: "It is a time when all things flourish." And, as Wilhelm says, there is rapid, easy progress. The question for a person using the I Ching as a fresh perspective on their life and their circumstances is, what does the commentary tell us?

Richard Wilhelm's Christianity is evident but, as this was my introduction to the I Ching, and I had come out of a Christian context, it was helpful. He often offered analogies by quoting from the Bible, and because the quotations were familiar, it helped me. Has Wilhelm gone further, though, and warped the message of the I Ching?

It took me some time to imbibe the concepts of the I Ching. The concepts and images form a different package to Christianity, both in content and context. Gradually, they enter into the way one thinks. It seems a harsh judgement to say that Wilhelm has warped the real meaning of the I Ching. Everyone who works with the I Ching comes from a particular perspective, a particular set of experiences, skills and blind spots. This is in the nature of human beings.

Gradual development can be characterised as a snake that sheds its skin when the time comes, and in its life this will happen many times. When I obtained Alfred Huang's book, it was as if I shed the skin of Richard Wilhelm and learned something new. But the metaphor is not quite good enough, because I had not shed Richard Wilhelm at all; I had augmented him with a different perspective. I was able to see where Huang offered me more – occasionally more, and often something different.

This happened every time I acquired a new book. I was like the richly endowed prince of hexagram 35, who received royal favours and was received in audience three times in one day.

8 Readings for circumstances

What I initially liked about the I Ching was that it was tailored to circumstances. There wasn't just the one set of sayings that were supposed to be true absolutely and in every circumstance.

Hexagram 35 shows the sun rising above the earth. It is a time of easy progress, and there are judgements that are relevant to the time. For example, although things are easy, remember to be humble, don't be tempted to do wrong, but do seize the opportunity and make the most of it. However, not all circumstances are like this. Times change.

35: Progress: Jing

When the circumstances are different, it may not be helpful to assume that progress will be easy. One may encounter conflict. We may be blocked and facing disputes. This is the case in hexagram 6. And this is not the only hexagram involving obstacles. There is also 12: Standstill/Hindrance, and 39: Obstruction/Hardship (using Wilhelm's and Huang's names). Broadly considered, there are other hexagrams as well, that relate to conflict and obstruction.

However, one does not use the I Ching in this way. One allows the coins to choose. One throws the coins six times and then sees what hexagram ensues (or if there are any moving lines, a second hexagram). The result can be unexpected, just as I found when I threw the hexagram 12: Peace, and was sacked the next day. One is then forced to take one's own all-important(!) perspective and see it in a larger context. This is what can be illuminating. Sometimes the learning can be hard.

Over time, we might also get to see how our perspective was limited, and we were not ready to change, even though the circumstances were hurting us. Subjecting ourselves to the hexagrams, we change. We come to enter the sphere of the I Ching. There are challenges and hazards, in life and in the process of facing the challenges. In 17: Following, Karcher says: Yield to the path set out before you. You are involved in a series of events that are firmly connected. Move with it. Your need to express yourself turns into self-cultivation.

In this hexagram, the trigram Thunder is below the trigram Lake. Karcher says this stirs up joyous ideas (Lake is Joy, and Thunder is Arousing), and it enables us to cleanse and renovate the images that weigh down our minds. The point of living is to liberate ourselves from our oppressive beliefs and attitudes, which may come from our childhood, to achieve an awareness of all-that-is.

My learning was not systematic. I dived in, throwing the coins regularly and reading what was said about the hexagrams in the various commentaries. What commentaries did I read? Once I realised there were many books on the I Ching, I began to buy them, to accumulate them, and to examine their differing perspectives. A few came from book fairs, and a few more came from bookshops, but the internet became a helpful source as well: both new books and second-hand books.

The throwing of the coins is an act of randomness, but then I had to decide which book to consult. Usually, when I acquired a new book, I would use it for a month or so, until I got the feel of it. Sometimes that was enough, and I put it away, but sometimes the book became part of the books I consulted regularly. Some of the books focus on society, politics and organisational life, while some are more concerned with social interaction, and some are concerned with personal decisions, self-awareness, and self-development.

Choosing a book to consult is another act of randomness. It is not systematic, but I do tend to rotate through about ten of the books, dipping into their different perspectives. It will probably be a long time until I have read the whole of every book. There are sixty-four hexagrams, but you may get one or more moving lines, which turns the hexagram into another hexagram, which means that there are over four thousand possibilities. It is like a plant pushing energetically up through the earth (the concept embodied in 46: Pushing Upward).

One time I asked the I Ching if it was obscure. I wasn't being flippant; it was a fair question. It gave me the hexagram 57: Gentle Penetration (made up of Wind upon Wind), and two moving lines, so it changed to 46: Pushing Upward (Wood: Rising up through Earth). Wilhelm's commentary on 57 said the wind disperses the clouds and leaves the sky serene. It works gradually and inconspicuously, but its influence never lapses, and its effects are enduring.

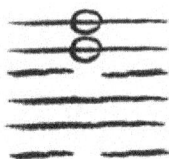

57: Gentle Penetration:
Xun

46: Pushing Upward: Sheng

For 46 it said there is vertical ascent from obscurity to the sun-power. One must see the Great Man (which could be seen as the I Ching itself). Heap up small things in order to achieve something great. Be devoted in character and do not be hasty. Simply continue, not pausing.

To learn the I Ching, you have to learn the trigrams; there are eight of them, and they have layers of meaning. A hexagram is made up of a lower trigram and an upper trigram. There is a need for a compendium, where the elements are presented in an orderly fashion, starting with how yin and yang build up to form the trigrams, describing the imagery of the eight trigrams, and then showing how the sixty-four hexagrams derive from pairs of trigrams.

There is more: the lines can be yin or yang, and they can be moving or still. Any moving lines change into their opposites, and so a new hexagram is formed.

The eight trigrams

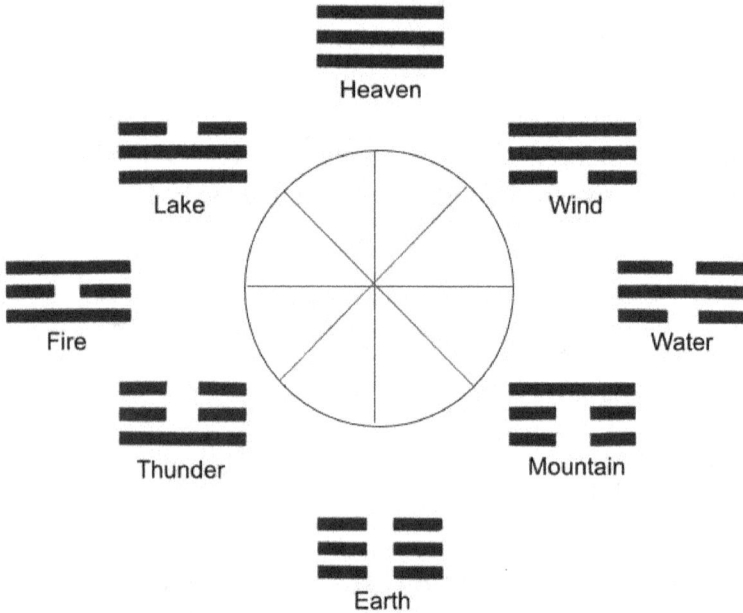

Heaven

Lake

Wind

Fire

Water

Thunder

Mountain

Earth

The first hexagram you receive, then the moving lines, and also the second hexagram, are all relevant to the question of your inquiry. Once you are familiar with how the trigrams form the hexagrams, you can work with this imagery.

There are other aspects. Some commentators explore where a hexagram sits in the sequence of hexagrams. Brightness: 30, which is Fire doubled, comes just after Darkness, or Abysmal: 29, which is Water doubled. 29 and 30 are the last two hexagrams in the Upper Canon (1 to 30), while 31 to 64 is called the Lower Canon. The Upper

Canon is about the workings of Heaven and Earth, while the Lower Canon is about humankind.

The universe begins with Heaven and Earth. Heaven is not the sky or the stars; it is the source of the Earth and everything in it. It is sublime and initiating. Earth is called receptive, responding and nurturing. These make up hexagrams 1 and 2. They start the Upper Canon.

Water and Fire come at the end of the Upper Canon because fire and water are the qualities of the things that have been formed on the Earth. They represent yin and yang in material form and in life. Finally, after all the changes that occur between 1 and 2, and 29 and 30, they resolve themselves into their final forms: Water is doubled, and Fire is doubled.

For Water, this is like plunging down a ravine: you have success in your heart, but in fact it is only your sincerity that keeps you safe. For Fire, this is continuing to be bright, persevering, illuminating the four corners of the world.

Where do the other doubled trigrams occur? They all occur in the Lower Canon. In a similar way, they are pairs with each other. Thunder doubled forms 51, and Mountain doubled forms 52. It is easy to see that they belong together and balance each other, because Thunder shakes things up and Mountain is a symbol of stillness. Thunder shakes the ground up in a spring storm, when it brings life awake again after winter. It might shake us out of our lethargy. Mountain is stillness, an image of calmness after agitation. It is also a vision of seeing clearly from a high point.

The last doubled hexagrams are 57 and 58, again, the same trigram paired with each itself. 57 is Wind. The I Ching has the image of a gentle, penetrating wind which brings success. It denotes persistence. It also denotes a commander whose manner is gentle but firm; his orders are spread abroad. 58 is Joyous, Lake. True joy rests on firmness and yielding within. It is infectious, but it does not degenerate into uncontrolled mirth. (Wilhelm expresses it this way.)

One question that this account leaves unanswered is about the hexagrams at the start and end of the Lower Canon. None of the doubled hexagrams sit there. The four hexagrams concerned are 31 and 32, and 63 and 64. The explanation here will not delve into the trigrams. This is best done when all the trigrams are explored.

The first two hexagrams (31 and 32) concern courtship and marriage; 31 is Mutual Influence, or Wooing, while 32 is Duration, Long-Lasting, or Marriage. After all the beings have come into existence, male and female are distinguished and there comes the relationship of husband and wife. The other relationships in life follow: parent and child, siblings, ruler and official, and finally, friends. And there is guidance for these situations.

The last two hexagrams in the Lower Canon are 63: After Completion, and 64: Before Completion. The order is not a mistake. The message is that after every ending there comes a new beginning. We might seek to ascend to the top of a mountain and stay there, enjoying our pre-eminence, but the I Ching says this is not the nature of life. Things have their peak and they disintegrate, and we should not be bitter about this. We learn how to make things endure, but we should be sensible enough to do this without false expectations about the natural way of things.

Wilhelm says "After Completion, success in small matters. Perseverance furthers. At the beginning, good fortune. At the end, disorder." For Before Completion, he says "the superior man is careful in the differentiation of things, so that each fulfils its place."

9 Books on the I Ching

After the Wilhelm-Baynes' edition of the I Ching was released in 1950, it seeped into modern culture, although it was already known by some people in the West. The German mathematician and philosopher Leibniz (born 1646) was familiar with it. He was exploring the binary system of numbers: 0 and 1, yin and yang. The Danish physicist Neils Bohr, born 1885, had thought about the I Ching as a parallel to his work in physics.

A number of modern musicians dabbled with it: John Cage, Bob Dylan, George Harrison; and writers: Herman Hesse, Douglas Adams, Allen Ginsberg. The I Ching has made its appearance in several movies, for example, "You've Got Mail" (1998).

Carl Jung commented, in Richard Wilhelm's 1950 publication, that "The method of the I Ching does indeed take into account the hidden individual quality in things and men, and in one's own unconscious self as well". Herman Hesse said, "I have been inspired by the wisdom of China. The I Ching can transform life."

The sixty-four hexagrams were considered by their ancient authors to be a fully adequate interpretation of every human situation at any given moment during an individual's life.

Since Wilhelm and Legge, many people have attempted to produce a tailored edition of the I Ching. Joel Biroco did a review of the available books in 1995; it is still posted on a website. There are more new books as at 2024, and some of the books he reviewed are no longer available. He lists almost seventy books, of which I possess about twenty. On the other hand, I have about twenty books that he does not list; many of these are newish.

Biroco starts with the Wilhelm/Baynes edition. He calls it "The definitive English translation; from Chinese into German by Wilhelm, into English by Baynes. Wilhelm was in prolonged contact with the oral tradition at the very end of the Imperial era, via his teacher Lao Nai-Hsüan. He was the right man in the right place at the right time; this is not something that can be re-done, no matter how good fresh translations are. As Carl Jung put it, it is as if this book 'delivered the last message of the old, dying China to Europe'…. The quality of the language used is superb; it rates as a work of literature".

Biroco comments on the books he reviews and on their authors. At times he is acerbic. For example, of one book he says: "The author is disenchanted with the 'obscure symbolism' of the Chinese text and dismisses it as ancient irrelevance. This couldn't be more misguided." Some books he regards as "a fair introduction for the beginner", but they lack detail for serious use.

Of another version, "The I Ching: The No. 1 Success Formula" he says, "Despite the trashy title, the overall judgments are quite well written and the old Chinese illustrations charming." One book he accuses of having a haughty tone. Of another he says, "His interpretations of difficult situations veer towards looking on the black side".

Of another book, "The Executive I Ching", he is scathing: "Pathetic. He invents a tycoon's tarot with wordings that have echoes of the I Ching. An executive toy for random decision-making."

Yet another book also draws his ire: "Modern Interpretation of the Ancient I Ching": "No interpretation at all. The most blatant re-spray of Wilhelm I have yet encountered. This book was published in the Far East and is imported by Chinatown bookshops, which may lead some to imagine it is authentic."

Nor is he too kind with another, called "I Ching for Beginners". He says, it is undoubtedly written from her experience of being one".

For a book called "I Ching – The Hexagrams Revealed" he merely notes that the book does not include the lines for each hexagram, so it is not much use.

Another author actually turned the I Ching into a Tarot deck, calling it "The I Ching of the Goddess". Biroco merely notes that "It sounds preposterous". Another author turned it into "A Woman's Book of Reclaiming". For example, all the solar imagery is changed into the moon. But there is no sun. Biroco describes it as a shallow attempt to exploit a readership.

An unusual author was Khigh Alx Dhiegh (1910–1991). He was an actor of mixed ancestry who appeared in many movie and television shows, including as the arch villain Wo Fat in "Hawaii Five-O". Dhiegh stated that his mother was Chinese, Spanish, English and Egyptian, and his father was Italian, Portuguese and Zulu.

He developed an interest in the I Ching when he was in his twenties, and eventually became Director of the International I Ching Studies Institute and Rector of the Taoist Sanctuary in Los Angeles. He was the author of new commentary on the I Ching which is called *The Eleventh Wing*. This is to say, its intention is to add to the Ten Wings of commentary provided by Confucius around 500 BC: a bold assertion.

Biroco notes that Mr Dhiegh constructed and patented I Ching study aids; Biroco also said he had found the original patent for the I Ching-Dex machine that Mr Dhiegh invented.

I do have a copy of Deigh's book. I found it in a library in Sydney recently, and then successfully ordered it from an American online bookshop. It was published in 1973.

Dhiegh believed in a ritual approach to the I Ching. The throw of the coins might be inherently random, but the process ought not be careless or hasty. People can be more or less ceremonious about this procedure, but one aims to be calm and clear. Given this perspective, there does not seem to be much need for ancillary devices; the procedure is simple enough. Three coins are sufficient for the purpose, and an appropriate small container in which to store them, and a cloth on which to throw the coins.

The most effort needs to lie in considering how the hexagram relates to your situation. One needs to see one's life in a larger perspective. It becomes a question of how you expect life to interact with you, and what you expect from it.

10 Journey of the I Ching to the West

It is necessary to tell the story of how the I Ching came to be, and how it came down to us through history. It did not migrate out from China until the 1600s, when the first Christian missionaries went overseas from Europe to win converts. However, the mission to bring cultural treasures back to Europe was more successful than the mission to spread Christianity.

Wilhelm says it can safely be said that the seasoned wisdom of several thousand years has found its way into the I Ching. Conversely, its wisdom has found its way into Confucianism and Taoism, which both originated around 500 BC. Quotations from the I Ching used to decorate Chinese homes. The I Ching also gave rise to an extensive literature of the occult, and a deep layer of tradition enshrouded the I Ching for many centuries. Wilhelm says that Western scholars often bowed to layers of superstition, thinking of the ancient Chinese as primitive peoples.

In the beginning, the Book of Changes was a set of oracles used to make pronouncements to decide questions about what would happen – in harvest, in weather, in war. James Legge gives the origin of the I Ching as a myth.

The myth is that the eight trigrams were invented by the Emperor Fu Hsi, who is said to have lived from 2,953 to 2,838 BC, although some more recent writers have dated him to 8,000 BC and even 12,000 BC. He was the first of the Five Emperors, and he was the father of civilisation. He is said to have been miraculously conceived by his mother, who carried him for twelve years. He taught his people to hunt, fish, keep flocks, and make fire. He showed them how to split the wood of trees, to twist silk threads, and to stretch silk to make musical instruments.

From the markings on the back of a tortoise, Fu Hsi created the eight trigrams and their imagery, and these became the basis of divination for the next thousand years, transmitted orally. However, more than divination, the rudiments of the I Ching were used to teach and guide people, to teach ethics, and to impart a sense of the universe and its origin.

Around 1,150 BC, at the end of the Shang dynasty, King Wen was imprisoned by the cruel and corrupt Shang Emperor. While he was in gaol, he conceived how the eight trigrams could be doubled to make hexagrams, and thus the sixty-four hexagrams (8 x 8) were created. King Wen ushered in the Chou (Zhou) Dynasty.

King Wen and his son, the Duke of Chou, augmented the sixty-four hexagrams with the names and the judgements for all the hexagrams. (According to some scholars, King Wen named the sixty-four hexagrams and the Duke of Chou wrote the text for all of the individual lines (6 x 64). This new form of the I Ching became the foundation for philosophy, metaphysics and morals.

However, there is also a supplementary text consisting of commentaries and appendices, which is called the Ten Wings, added hundreds of years later. These have been attributed to Confucius (551-479 BC), although there is some controversy about this.

This version of history does not claim to be the unequivocal truth. It suggests the shape of the I Ching's history. It offers to be helpful for someone who is seeking to understand the imagery and the import of the I Ching. As Hua-Ching Ni says, "Self-cultivation creates a firm, calm power. The constancy of your efforts will cause the wisdom of your soul to shine through".

11 A story with an I Ching perspective

To start using the I Ching, it may help to indulge in a little triangulation. What if you read a story that incorporated the I Ching as commentary? Then there would be three things: the story, the readings from the I Ching, and a commentary. Years ago, I did this in a back-to-front way. I had not written a story before; my piles of writing were all non-fiction (employment law, management commentary and the like). But there was a story I wanted to write, only I thought it had to be written as history, that is, as non-fiction.

The story was dramatic, and true. It had involved six years of my life as a manager in a disability services organisation. It is said that sometimes, such contexts can be vicious. I had good success for several years but then the tide turned. I didn't understand what was going on at the time, but the Head Office of the organisation in Sydney began to attack me. We were seven hundred kilometres away from Sydney, so it seemed a bit gratuitous and inordinately intense. They seemed to be out for the kill.

While I was the manager, I used the I Ching (privately). I would ask it questions and it would give me perspectives. It was helpful. It was also how I wanted to live. After I got the sack (yes, it was as preposterous as that) and things fell apart, I walked off and pursued other interests, as they say politely.

However, the story sat there, waiting to be told. It sat in the background for about twenty years, until one of my sons said to me, "Don't write it as a history. Write it as a story." Sometimes the obvious suddenly becomes obvious. I didn't know how I could do it: it was over twenty years ago, and I had very little in the way of notes.

And yet, the story took shape almost effortlessly. As I was writing, I remembered people and events, and the flow of it.

What does this have to do with the I Ching? I didn't have any notes; recall, I used to write on pieces of paper, and then after a while I lost them or threw them out. In 2009, when I decided on writing the story of it, there were none of these notes left. But I took a brave step. I thought, if I trust the I Ching, I could throw the coins now, while I am in the process of writing the book. This time, I will keep the readings and include them in the book. It was not Wilhelm's edition that I used; it was Wu Wei's. I know some people might frown on this, but often I found his version to be surprisingly apt.

Biroco rubbished it in his review, but for different reasons. He said it had a completely fabricated aura of authenticity. It mimicked the cover of Wilhelm's 1950 book. Biroco showed a picture of the cover. I, too, was shocked at this brazen opportunism. However, so disgusted was Biroco with the cover that he did not look at the inside.

The edition I bought in Kuala Lumpur in 2006 had been published later (it was my first visit overseas; it was exciting to see the Kinokuniya Bookshop there; I was familiar with it from Sydney), and the cover was different. It was distinctive, and very attractive: nice images and nice colours. This edition of the book was called *The Book of Answers*, which I thought was a little presumptuous, but despite this, I found the text to be quite thoughtful and insightful.

The book I ended up writing on my turbulent experience as a manager is interspersed with hexagrams from the I Ching. Towards the end is when I got the sack, after six years. No dishonesty, no collapse in finances, no incompetence; just concocted, snide inferences, and bullying.

One chapter is below, after I got the sack. The hexagrams are shown as well. Note that when you throw the coins, you can get either unchanging lines or moving lines. If any of the lines are moving, you read the first hexagram, read the moving lines, then change the moving lines into their opposites, so you get the second hexagram. This means that the situation is changing. In the chapter shown below, you can see how this happens.

Extract from *The Ten Thousand Things*, 2011, Glenn Martin

Chapter 43: Abatement of danger

I went home and stayed there. I stayed and stayed. Trish came to my house a couple of times, but I didn't have much to say to her. I was standing still, and I didn't know how long I would do that.

I was thinking about "business". I was thinking about whether I was someone else who had been disguised as a manager. And if so, who was that other person? I was thinking about the bigness of my roof, and how I was just one person, alone, under that roof. I wasn't sure if I would move again, or if anything else would move. But nor was I trying to make anything move. I would just stand still until. Until.

With some effort, with some heaviness, I threw the I Ching again. I would see.

I sat on the floor, all my books around me, witnesses, sages. For this I chose the version by Wu Wei, a recent addition to my library. I would describe it as lucid and pastoral. It writes a simple pathway through the obscure and the arcane, like a wise father. He calls his book, *The Book of Answers*. Bold.

Again, I was surprised. The first hexagram had a moving line, so it generated a second hexagram, and both hexagrams were about forming and working with groups. Ts'ui (45): Gathering Together, was followed by P'i (8): Joining, Supporting, Uniting.

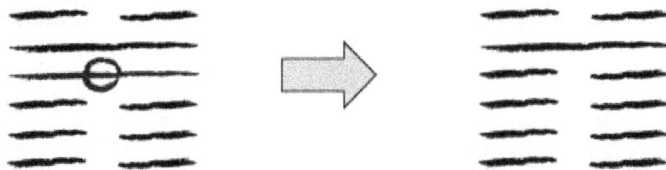

45: Gathering Together:
Ts'ui

8: Uniting: P'i

Ts'ui, the more I thought about it, was a retrospective on my time in the organisation. Wu Wei's commentary summarised what my endeavour had been about over the last six years. All the elements were there: have a well-defined cause that will draw all the members together and earn their support; be enthusiastic about your goal; show that your goal is meaningful and worthwhile.

As a leader, be sincere, strong, and dedicated to the group's well-being. Your motives must be ethical, moral, and rooted in an inner desire, not just to meet your own needs, but to be of service to the members and those outside the group. Develop clear-cut guidelines for achieving your goal, then move, always, in the direction of your goal. Your followers rely on you to set an example, and you must show them that you are tireless, dedicated, enthusiastic and loyal.

Wu Wei finished his prescription for the leader by saying "You will be called upon to make sacrifices to obtain your goal." I could not see how I had obtained my goal. I didn't for a moment believe Barry's crude accusation ("You've stuffed it up big time") and I didn't think I could have done much about the machinations of the organisation's central office – clearly there was an agenda that I still didn't understand. But in all of that, there was no doubt things were in a mess, and I had lost any active part in the course of events.

There was something else that Wu Wei said: "The group will have its own goals and reasons for its existence, but you must be clear about your own personal goal." I remembered that I did have a personal

49

goal when I started. I wanted to learn about what it took to be a manager and a leader.

Why? I didn't know at the time, and I still didn't know, but I had been clear that that was the goal.

So, ask yourself again, did you achieve your personal goal? Well, did I achieve it if everything has fallen apart? Doesn't that mean I didn't learn? I went to the second hexagram, P'i. Wu Wei said, "The hexagram represents a time when you can easily gather people around you and form a group. The group can be as small as yourself or much larger. The pronouncement of this kua (hexagram) is that forming a group or being part of a group will bring you good fortune."

Even if I didn't understand all of this, there was one clear message: start moving. Do not stand still any longer. The commentary went on, "Look to strengthening and improving your character so that you are always performing at optimum levels. Before you begin, inquire of the oracle again, and ask what you need to know to accomplish your goal."

I was wrestling with the idea that had been presented to me about forming a group. I was still staring at the ashes of the last one. But if this was a retrospective comment on my involvement with the organisation, then I had this comment to consider: If you begin without being equal to the task you will incur misfortune, and it would have been better for you if you had never attempted the task.

I concluded that I would accept the invitation to inquire again. This time I would take on the question it had suggested: what do I need to know to accomplish my goal?

I got the hexagram Hsieh (40): Abatement of Danger. It had two moving lines, and it transformed to Ting (50): The Cauldron.

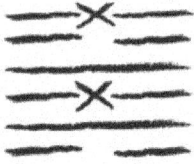

40: Abatement of Danger:
Hsieh

50: The Cauldron: Ting

I knew what Ting was; it was the source of nourishment for the people. It was the holy offering, the dispensation of spiritual knowledge and wisdom. Supreme good fortune and success. Wu Wei says, in order to dispense great spiritual wisdom, you must first possess it, so you must seek it.

Of course I had learned about being a manager and leader. I was still learning, even in my isolation, my standing still. I was weaving the wind, conducting in absentia. The pieces were still falling into place. Nothing I did had been wrong. It may have been wrong in a superficial sense. For example, it may not have been tactful to tell the CEO to mind her own business, but when I said that, I was absolutely sure that this was the right thing to say to her, that this was exactly what needed to be said, and it hit the spot. This was not two managers muttering platitudes to each other; this was psychic warfare.

Had I lost? The arcs of cause and effect run wide. The Dalai Lama, following the Tibetan Buddhism tradition, calls it dependent origination. This conception sees reality as an infinite and indefinite series of interrelated causes and conditions of which we are but part. Everything that exists is part of this web, and every action has this universal dimension.

We do not know where our actions end. What we need to know is that our actions do most good in the world when we are firm and correct, when our lives countenance joy and right action.

The other hexagram, Hsieh (40), was also intriguing. "The danger subsides. If your question concerns the taking of action, taking that action will cause the danger to completely dissipate, thus bringing good fortune." At first, I couldn't think of any actions I could take, or needed to take. I had been effectively taken out of the situation with my dismissal.

The message was persistent, however. Reflect carefully on the entire situation. Avoid spending too much time deliberating. Too much reflection cripples the power of decision. Eventually I thought of two things I could do.

The first was, I would talk to the person I had met who was on the board of the organisation's central office, and who was also president of the organisation in one of the neighbouring towns. I didn't know if he would speak with me at all, but I would ask him. What had happened to our local organisation should no longer be thought of as an isolated instance. The "entire situation" was the total organisation over which the central office held legal power.

The second thing I could do was simple. I would go to town. I had been avoiding being in public. I had been closeting myself, going to town only to buy food, and getting away quickly before too many people saw me. Okay, I would stop that. I would go to town and be prepared to be seen. I would stand up straight. It didn't matter if some people had got the idea I was an incompetent manager, or dishonest.

I would be seen, standing and walking tall.

*   *   *   *   *

I think it is fair to say the book was well-received. As far as I could see, none of the dishonest, vicious people in the situation were punished, but it also seemed to me that they had all disappeared in about two years. In hexagram 6: Conflict, one is cautioned to refrain from attempting to achieve a victory that is completely crushing. The appropriate end, rather, is peace and harmony.

I suppose that people who struggled with the idea of the I Ching may have found it an intrusion into the story, but people who were really interested in the story did not seem to be put off.

12 My I Ching journals and the eight trigrams

Back in my younger years I took advice from the I Ching when I was in difficulty. Yes, usually in difficulty, feeling oppressed but not sure what to do. In one notebook I found notes from 1988. The first reading was one hexagram changing to another: 29, Abyss, changing to 64, Before Completion. That was dramatic. At first, the situation appears like the abyss, and you fear you will be swallowed up in it. But then it resolves itself. It is not like deliverance; rather, it is all the parts coming together, bringing a story to completion. The story was there, and it had momentum and meaning. It just needed to be drawn to its conclusion.

The next reading I wrote in the book was a month later. It was 38: Disunion, changing to 14: Abundance. And this is another dramatic turnaround. In Disunion, Fire is above Lake. Fire moves upward and Lake moves downward. Things are moving apart, so there is success only in small things. "All beings diversify, but their functions are the same."

The first hexagram changed to 14, which is Abundance or Great Harvest. Fire is above Heaven. This is sublimely smooth and prosperous.

I think that in those days I was too anxious for things to move on, for the Abundance to arrive and the Disunion to be gone. Nowadays

I think I might try to slow things down a bit, to see what I should notice and what I could learn.

You could ask whether I became dependent on the I Ching. For the past few years, I have used it regularly and written down notes. Does it mean that I defer my thinking and my decisions until I have seen what the I Ching has to say? Surely this is a bad thing, not a good thing. One of the I Ching commentators referred to having done this in his younger life, running home to throw the coins. Yet, the I Ching speaks. It comments, one way or another.

I ponder about whether I use the I Ching too often. Khigh Alx Dhiegh says that, as with all potentially powerful processes, the I Ching should not be utilised too often. Most of life's decisions can be made by reflecting on one's alternatives, thinking about what one has learned from past experience, and combining these thoughts with one's subjective feeling about the course to follow. He says the I Ching is best used when there is conflict between thoughts and feelings, or when none of the alternatives appear to be workable.

To push this discussion a little further, Dhiegh talks about causality. From the planning, organised, hard-knowledge perspective, causality is the web of life. It connects causes to effects and makes up the flow of the world. Certainly there is order in the world; if it were completely random, there would be no relationships between things. But if things were completely determined, a person would have no freedom or choice.

The I Ching recognises the potential for chance to play a part, just as it recognises there are times when things are amenable to change. The appropriate thing to do then is to cooperate in the process of change. Part of the process of using the I Ching is to tune into feeling, to be aware of it and consider how one needs to act or respond to a situation. This opens the full spectrum of possibilities for human action. Carl Jung, in his Foreword to Wilhelm's book, says the Western mind carefully sifts, selects, isolates and weighs, whereas the Chinese mind encompasses everything in the moment.

Times differ. Sometimes one will encounter 29: The Abyss (Water upon Water). Perhaps a better name is Ravine. The image is of water pouring down a ravine. In this situation the water can only do one thing: to continue to pour down the ravine, using its inherent energy, not fighting it at all. With sincerity one will survive and flourish. Nor is one brash or a bully. One simply does what one must do in the situation.

This situation can be contrasted to where one encounters a body of water and wishes to go across – to cross the great stream (64: Before Completion). It is dangerous and one has to be sure one can accomplish it. But then, our path has led us to the edge of the stream.

When we use the I Ching we are open to what happens. It is not in anyone's scheming to affect what occurs. The coins deliver their verdict and we go to the appropriate hexagram(s). There is something simple about this situation; not complex. It is not through our cleverness that we take notice, or resolve things.

And then we may note that some commentators call the I Ching a philosophical psychology. The ancient sages saw humans as inseparable from the cosmos. Humans are a microcosm that perfectly replicates the macrocosm and reflects awareness of it. The medium for the play of the moment into the question asked of the I Ching is the play of the eight trigrams, each of which embodies an element of nature. King Wen and the Duke of Chou resolved that all the types of situations that a human could face were represented by the interactions of the eight trigrams with each other, making sixty-four hexagrams.

This is to say, the eight trigrams are images of all that happens in heaven and on earth. And they are in a state of continual transition, one changing into another, just as each phenomenon in the world is continually evolving. This is the fundamental concept of the I Ching. The trigrams are symbols for changing transitional states. Things are not static; hence, the trigrams are representations of tendencies in movement (as Wilhelm expresses it).

The eight images have manifold meanings. They represent certain processes in nature, having an inherent character. They stand for qualities (strong, joyful etc). They stand for the family (father, mother, first son, et cetera) and the functions of each.

Everything in life is addressed by the eight trigrams: Heaven, Thunder, Water, Mountain, Earth, Wind (or sometimes, Wood), Fire, Lake – and their interactions with each other.

The hexagrams give us the results of all the trigrams interacting with each other. One trigram is above, one trigram is below. In the hexagrams, the position of the trigrams is important. The trigrams are shown in the table.

The Eight Trigrams

Hexagram	Name	Description	Meanings	Images	Family relationship
	Qian	Heaven	Strong, Creative	Heaven	Father
	Kun	Receptive	Devoted, Yielding	Earth	Mother
	Zhen	Arousing	Movement	Thunder	First son
	Kan	Abysmal	Dangerous	Water	Second son
	Gen	Keeping Still	Resting	Mountain	Third son
	Xun	Gentle	Penetrating	Wind/ Wood	First daughter
	Li	Clinging	Light-giving	Fire	Second daughter
	Dui	Joyous	Joyful	Lake	Third daughter

The vision of the ancient people was a system of knowledge that enabled them to solve the problems in their lives. Living close to nature, they saw their first teacher as nature herself. They learned that she provides for and supports people, and they learned the laws of change. They learned that the laws of nature are also the laws of humanity, and so harmony is the key to life. The balanced way of life is the fundamental path.

In contrast, the rush of modern society and its feverish ambition obscure the ways of nature, which is still the true source of our lives. The I Ching is a friend. The eight trigrams are the eight helping spirits, each with its own energy. In any situation, two spirits interact, one active in the outer world, the other active in the inner world. The trigrams are in a given relation to each other. (In some situations, it is the one spirit doubled.) From the two trigrams comes the hexagram, and thus the judgement.

To learn the I Ching is a matter of knowledge and feeling. One must know the eight trigrams and their meanings, descriptions and images, and know how the sixty-four hexagrams are derived from the paired trigrams. One must also know how the moving lines change into their opposites, and identify the new hexagram. The most absorbing part of the practice is to consider your situation, and what the I Ching is saying to you about it. This may relate to your work life, your social life, your self-conceptions, your sense of peace or doubt, your attitudes towards other people, perhaps specifically, or your attitude towards any aspect of your behaviour.

The I Ching posits ideals for personal growth, and it always suggests how you can further the rhythm and harmony of life. Qian is the trigram Heaven, and Gen is the trigram Mountain. When Heaven is above Mountain, it forms Retreat (33: Dun). What is Retreat about? The attribute of Heaven is creative power; the attribute of Mountain is keeping still. Here, a sage confronts stillness and retreats. Inferior persons are advancing, and it is time for the wise to withdraw.

33: Retreat: Dun

Retreat is not flight. Flight is cowardice. It is a matter of waiting for the right time to advance. One can use retreat to preserve one's strength. It is favourable to be steadfast and upright. Prosperity and smoothness will eventuate. The six lines consider the process of retreat and how one might conduct oneself wisely during the six phases of retreat.

13 Moving lines and a minor stroke

The best thing I could do, from the beginning, was to get the feel of how the trigrams related to each other. They were all part of a single cohesive system. There is movement and there are persistent conditions, but on closer scrutiny, things are constantly in flux, and this is reflected in the fact that the hexagrams comprise both firm and yielding lines. When changes reach a certain point, they become visible and bring about transformations.

These changes are subject to laws. The eight trigrams succeed one another by turns, the firm and the yielding lines displacing one another over the cycles of time. Simplicity arises out of pure receptivity. The sage follows what is simple and thereby fulfils what is possible in the spatial world. Thus he can endure for long, and win adherence to the path of simplicity and love. He is free of confusing conflicts. By means of the easy and simple we grasp the laws of the entire world.

The easy and the simple are symbolised by very slight changes in the individual lines. It is an easy movement. The divided lines become undivided, and the undivided lines become divided. Thus the laws of all processes under heaven are depicted, and perfection can be obtained.

As Huang expresses it, "The purpose of the I Ching is to offer guidance for favourable action in one's life, and at the same time to avoid misconduct that invites misfortune."

There is an orchestration of the trigrams that is mysterious to us, but to know the meaning of the trigrams is to be able to move through life effortlessly.

The first, second and third sons that Wilhelm refers to are trigrams with one unbroken, male (yang) line, the line moving up from the first to the second and the third position.

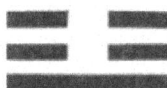      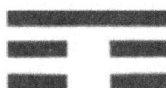

Thunder   Water   Mountain

The first, second and third daughters are trigrams with one broken (yin) line, with the line moving up from the bottom to the second then the third position.

Wind   Fire   Lake

The male lines represent the danger of movement in its various stages. The female lines represent devotion and tranquillity. The yin and yang energies are constantly changing, seeking harmony.

Because every one of the lines can be a moving line, there are over 4,000 possibilities when you throw the I Ching coins (64 x 63).

This sequence happened. The first hexagram was Thunder above Earth; this is 16: Enthusiasm, also called Delight. There was one moving line, the top (sixth) line, so the hexagram changed to Fire above Earth, 35: Progress, also called Proceeding Forward, or Flourishing.

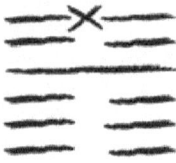

16: Enthusiasm: Yu   35: Progress: Jing

I was taking stock of myself after maybe having a minor stroke a few days ago. My experience was of having a headache all day, and the sight in my right eye being fuzzy in the middle of the field of vision. I wondered whether I was losing my personal equilibrium and whether everything I thought and did was wrong. I am expecting to work on this issue day by day, not for the question to be resolved in an instant. But I needed some assurance.

Importantly, the different commentators on the I Ching bring very different perspectives. I decided to read Stephen Karcher's *Total I Ching*. It digs into myth and draws on spirit. It can be a wild ride. I start with the image: Thunder above Earth. Thunder explodes, shaking the earth. But there is delight in it. The earth is coming back to life in spring. Karcher talks about great reserves of power and grace. How does one respond? One responds directly. He refers to a great being who responds to the command of heaven.

In martial arts, one cultivates the ability to react appropriately without thought, bypassing the slower processes of the mind that want to stand back and judge first. One is confident and moves smoothly, not just with power, but also with grace. Spirit manifests in quake and thunder, and it puts itself at the service of the earth's altar.

My default reaction is to stop and doubt.

The moving line at the top talked of the shadow world: a waning moon, a cave. But you can find out what you need and climb out of the cave.

The change was to 35: Flourishing. The sun is above the earth; emerge into the light. There is joy and delight. You are given gifts of horses that multiply. In one day you are received three times in audience. Emerge into the full light of day. Help things to flourish; be calm in your strength. Brighten power and virtue. Bright omens arise from the field. Earth below yields and sustains.

I don't regard my medical episode, whatever it was, as something completely beyond my power. I am part of it so, "emerging into the full light of day" is something I can choose to do or not do, accept or reject. My attitude makes a major difference. Some actions are favourable, as Huang says, and others are not. Earth below yields and sustains.

What part has Stephen Karcher played in my drama? He has entered into the world of the trigrams, the world created by Fu Hsi, and the application of the trigrams to human situations over five thousand years, and the reworking that King Wen carried out, and his son, the Duke of Zhou to create the hexagrams. And again, the thousands of years of application of this expanded commentary, its immersion in history and cultural events. And through it, the thread of the meaning of our existence. It is not a trivial thing.

14 Richard Rudd describes hexagram 16

On another day I obtain the hexagram 16 with no moving lines.

So, I read what Richard Rudd has to say. There is only a chance of about 1.5% that I will get a hexagram with no moving lines, and there is only a further chance of one in sixty-four that I will get the hexagram 16. Richard Rudd says that humans live in a great complex that spans vast time, and we are immersed in evolutionary changes. Our bodies and our consciousness are geared for evolution through our DNA, but we are also in shadow. We have dark clouds of fear that cause us to act in ways that the I Ching would say invite trouble.

Each hexagram is a representation of a shadow and a possibility. The possibility is a gift, and a source of bliss. And we are not powerless; we have the choice to live open-hearted. Each of the hexagrams is called a Gene Key. What is 16? It is a passage from Indifference to Versatility to Mastery. This is a strange concatenation of concepts.

Collectively, humans tend to act in indifference. Our fear causes us to put up a wall against our feelings. We feel it is better to be indifferent than to be exposed to the possibility of hurt. This means that we often avoid trying. It is better to be mediocre than to put all your effort into doing something that might fail. This means that we are often not even sure what we are good at. But we are comfortable, and everything is familiar.

Rudd expresses it harshly: "The opposite of life is not death but indifference." It leads to the diffusion of responsibility. It leads to pipe dreams: we may have the idea that we want to become something, but it will never be put to the test. The opposite? To do what you love, to follow a dream. And the image for this is thunder, being shaken up. (Richard Rudd's account is a vast extension of the I Ching's perspective.)

There is an energy to it that does not let others tread on you and stop you. The opinions of naysayers do not stand in your way. And you do not compromise yourself.

In this state, you begin to develop mastery. Developing skills opens up your talents. You discover there is a singular, unique consciousness within you, and when it is put to the service of humanity, it develops and becomes fulfilled. You acquire techniques, but you also move beyond techniques. Things become effortless. Other gifts become available to you, so you become versatile. And there is a different energy associated with this kind of activity; it is fed and rewarded from the environment. Things come to fulfilment, uniquely.

Rudd says this capacity is dormant in our body, a possibility that can unfold in us genetically. Ultimately it is associated with bliss. He uses the Hindu word "siddhi".

Elsewhere, Rudd says, "Thus the great cosmic drama unfolds, and every individual moves through progressive revelations before arriving at the ultimate revelation. The consciousness within form always has a story to follow. The trick is to fall in love with your own story and follow it without holding anything back. Two things are then assured – firstly, you will arrive at the story's end, and secondly, your story will be utterly unique and unlike anyone else's (Rudd, 2009, p. 265).

Delving into the I Ching, I accept that life is complex, but it is not an intellectual problem. Rudd also says, "You need to be a lover with a beginner's mind rather than arriving as an expert determined to solve a riddle." The thread at the centre is story: change always has a story it is following, and the thing to do is to follow the story.

15 Regulating life through the I Ching

What happens if you throw the I Ching every day? Does the stream of readings make sense? Does it flow? On one day I threw 3: Beginning, followed by 60: Regulation.

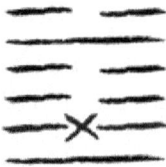

3: Beginning: Zhun   60: Regulation: Jie

I wend my way among the various books that I use. I guess I am making my own story from among what is offered. Beginning is called "Difficulty at the Beginning" by Wilhelm. His explanation is that when the world comes into being, lots of things are being created, life is prolific, many forms of life are trying to get a foothold, so it is chaotic. And the point of life is to bring order into this chaos so that it can fulfil its potential.

So I have to ask the question: in what sense am I at the beginning? As an outsider would see me, I am well down the track; perhaps I am even towards the end of it. My hair is grey.

But the I Ching says life is a series of beginnings and endings, and every ending is followed by a new beginning. Perhaps it is a job, or a task, or a project, or a relationship. These are periods of time when something develops and comes to fulfilment, and then it ceases or fades away. And all beginnings have their challenges. Clouds gather and rain falls. There is thunder. And yet, at the same time, there is growth.

The commentator that I read said: "The wise man does not attempt the mountain pass at this time. He consolidates his present position. He knows the storm will pass. To defy the storm directly would bring ruin. Better to wait."

Following this was Limitation: 60. This is not limitation that is imposed from the outside; it is self-imposed. Another name for limitation is regulation. It is how one regulates one's behaviour. Limits, regulations, rules, are ways of confronting the vastness of all-that-is. It is like bamboo: the length of a stick of bamboo is divided into short sections, separated by nodes. The effect is to make the stick of bamboo stronger, much stronger.

There is a caution in the use of limitation as well. One should not be so severe in limitation that it causes pain or impairment. Extremes lead to collapse.

So, I continue. Around me there is a profusion of life, at all stages: juvenile, developing, maturing, fading. In the midst of this profusion, it is best that one retains balance and confidence, being alert but joyful. That is all.

16 Shaken but not defeated

On another day I am shaken by circumstance, but I don't feel defeated. I will persevere. It is as if I don't know if the flood will cover my head or not. There are different stances towards such a position. Perhaps it would be wise to run, to show haste, to abandon the field. Some people might say, "Didn't you see the problems looming?"

Perhaps I thought of the flood because of the hexagram 60, Limitation. There, the Water is above the Lake. The lake forms a natural limit for the water, avoiding the destructiveness of the flood. It shows the need for limits.

But the I Ching tells me, 52: Still: Mountain upon Mountain. Then it says, 20: Watching, Tower: Wind over Earth.

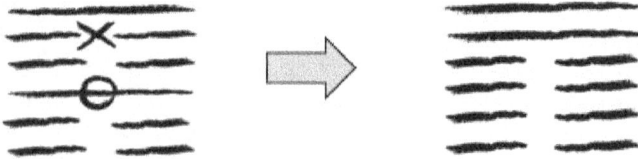

52: Keeping Still: Gen   20: Watching: Guan

Wilhelm says one stills the body and moves one's consciousness away from the body, allowing it to be calm. The bustle of circumstance fades, with its fears and agitated hopes. It is meditation.

John Minford, who has a wonderful grasp of the authenticity of Richard Wilhelm, says, "When time is still, be still. When time moves, move with it. The Tao is bright. The body sustains no harm. The true gentleman's thoughts do not stray beyond his proper position."

He also says, "The myriad things are completed", and I think back to 3: Beginning.

Yin dominates and forms the centre. After Stillness there is Watching. Watching is important if one is to live a worthwhile life. One must observe in order to understand. One must understand before one acts. One must consider different points of view in order to be balanced and unbiassed. The ancient kings visited the regions and observed the people. They obtained a larger view, beyond everyday life. Thus they were able to rule with wisdom.

The image is of the Wind blowing across the Earth. Minford says, "The wise man lets things go and cleaves to the Tao. He rules in the same way the wind moves across the earth, and there is peace. Non-action deepens the spiritual view."

Another writer says, "One achieves the Great Integrity in this way."

One is always stepping along the edge of the known. It is suggestive, but you can't say you are the master of it. What is the Tao? This is the most difficult of subjects. It sounds like nonsense. "The Tao that can be told is not the eternal Tao. The name that can be named is not the eternal name. The nameless is the beginning of heaven and earth. The named is the mother of the ten thousand things. Ever desireless, one can see the mystery. Ever desiring, one can see the manifestation."

"Under heaven, all can see beauty as beauty only because there is ugliness. All can know good as good only because there is evil. Therefore having and not having arise together."

"Therefore the sage goes about doing nothing, teaching no-talking. Work is done, then forgotten."

"The Tao is an empty vessel; it is used but never filled."

"Retire when the work is done; this is the way of heaven."

"Working yet not taking credit, leading yet not dominating, this is the Primal Virtue."

"Cut doors and windows for a room: it is the holes that make them useful. Therefore profit comes from what is there, usefulness from what is not there."

"Accept misfortune as the human condition. What do I mean? Misfortune comes from having a body. Without a body, how could there be misfortune? Surrender yourself humbly; then you can be trusted to care for all things. Love the world as your own self; then you can truly care for all things."

"Knowing the ancient beginning is the essence of Tao."

The Tao is the Great Integrity.

17 Making the decision to leave a job

It was the last day of work for the year. I was tired of my job. I was doing the design for online education courses at a college. It wasn't my place to write the teaching material, but I was tired of the material that was being presented to me. In an online history course, the writers seriously described the Ten Commandments, the ones that were given to Moses on the mountain, as "suggestions" and "recommendations". No matter what your stance is on religion, you can't frame the Ten Commandments that way in a history course. It is ludicrous; it is embarrassing. And yet the writers objected to my questioning them about it.

I thought that I would leave the job early in the new year. The I Ching gave me 38: Opposition and then 54: Marrying Maiden.

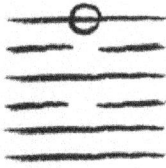

38: Opposition: Kui   54: Marrying Maiden: Gui Mei

In 38, Fire is above Lake, two elements that are moving apart. Fire is moving up, and Lake is moving down. My commentary said, misunderstandings occur. There is a divergence of interests. What was its advice? Cultivate your individuality and look around for compatriots. It advised me, "Do not attack; the stranger's demon dissolves in the rain."

Another commentary rounded out the picture: when the way of the Family comes to an end (the previous hexagram, 37, is Family), misunderstandings will occur. My view was that the college had functioned like a family a few years earlier, but that atmosphere had been eliminated in the pursuit of new goals. The commentary said change was natural and it would take its course. I felt that I would have to look elsewhere for new compatriots.

The second hexagram is a curious one: 54: Marrying Maiden. The commentary said, "Enter into service; fulfil your duty. Forget yourself for now; it is the end of an era. Bow your head humbly and accomplish tasks." It also said, through progress, one is sure to reach the place where one belongs. Understand the transitory from the perspective of the cosmic order of the universe, the larger picture. Pursue far-reaching goals and keep aware of the possibility of ruin.

Culturally, this is one of the most vexed hexagrams. It relates to customs of the ruling classes at the time when King Wen was writing the commentary. When a woman was given in marriage to a sovereign, often the woman's younger sister was given in marriage as well. She was the secondary bride, and she occupied a subsidiary position in the household. In the ideal case, the two women supported one another. Nevertheless, the second bride's position was one of inherent limitation.

The message is that the situation is not ideal, and to survive, one has to act humbly. King Wen himself was in a subsidiary position under the Shang dynasty. He was not in a position of power, and he could not afford to be outspoken.

And the I Ching was telling me that I was also in a subsidiary position, and it would not serve me well to be outspoken. I thought it was good advice. I left the job a month later, without fuss.

After these hexagrams, over the next few days I got 37: Family, and 36: Darkening of the Light. It was as if I was walking slowly backwards: 38, 37, 36. In both 37 and 36, the Fire is within. In 37 it is the hearth of home, while in 36 the Fire is covered by the earth. After the message about the unsavoury nature of my workplace, I was being told to care for the relationships at home, with the people who shared my living space and my activities, to take care of my dwelling. When the world outside is difficult, welcome and cultivate the safety of home.

On this foundation, one can find real directions in life, and one can depart from the past. Very often, the message of the I Ching is bold, and one must be bold within.

In 36, the earth covers the fire, but the fire is still burning; it has not gone out. In fact, at this time, you need the protection of the earth; you need to be hidden. Accept the difficulties of your journey. There are images for this hexagram that are omens. The sun below the earth is like a solar eclipse. It is emblematic of the struggle between the centres of power. An omen bird that cannot be seen calls from the darkness. Accept the mandate of this time.

Stephen Karcher's commentary is dramatic like this, and there are images that stick with you: a solar eclipse, an unexpected and oppressive period of darkness, and the singular cry of an unseen bird at an odd time.

70

18 Upon Water and the Lake

Most of my interaction with the I Ching seems to be a journey through metaphor. One day I got the hexagram 60: Water above Lake: Limitation or Regulation. The following day I got 47: Water below Lake: Exhaustion. What was that about? Water stands for flowing and danger, and structures dissolving. Lake stands for joy, contentment. I talked about 60: Limitation above. Here, the structure is in place and the emphasis is on maintaining the strengths that come with it.

In 47: Exhaustion, the lake is empty and there is distress. It is a matter of character, being able to hold firm when circumstances are not favourable. An example would be where you have something to say and it is not heard or believed. The wise person is aware of both the danger and the joy. Follow your will with perseverance. The difference is in the conditions; in one hexagram the Lake is below, while in the other it is above.

It shows that we have to be ever adaptable. Conditions are seldom static; they continue to change. The insight comes from within, and we are freed from oppression.

19 Hexagram 29: Water doubled

It is helpful to examine the hexagrams made up of doubled trigrams. This gives an indication of the nature of each trigram. I got 29: Abyss: Kan on New Year's Day: Water upon Water. Recall the image: water plunges down a ravine. In this situation it is not helpful to resist; one must flow onwards like a river. "Be the river." Success is in your heart. Keep going, although it is through dangerous places. Walk in lasting virtue. Be sincere and truthful. Carry on the business of teaching. And we must not forget that water is life-giving. Deeds will be honoured.

When one accepts the very nature of water, there will be success. Water does not seek to go up; it takes the lowest path. The *Tao Te Ching* says, "Under heaven nothing is softer or more yielding than water, yet for attacking the solid and strong, nothing is better.

"The highest good is like water. Water gives life to the ten thousand things and does not strive.

"Why is the sea the king of a hundred streams? Because it lies below them. Therefore it is the king of a hundred streams.

"The softest thing in the universe overcomes the hardest thing in the universe."

Deng Ming-Dao says that if we are to find the meaning of life, we must enter the pit.

In Richard Rudd's account, our default position is in shadow, and here the shadow is Half-Heartedness. As we become aware, we learn the Gift of Commitment, and finally, the state of Siddhi is Devotion. All of these concepts we can relate to the idea of water plunging down a gorge. If one feels lack of trust in life, one tries to hold back, and that is half-heartedness, or lack of commitment.

To be able to overcome the shadow, one learns Commitment: to set goals and then to bring our energy to pursue those goals. With a strong sense of commitment, one has power and one can determine the correct direction for reaching the goal. And one final thing: luck favours those who are committed to their goals. But to pursue a gaol requires one to pursue the unknown: a goal is not a certain thing. And it requires perseverance, to follow through, determined to reach the goal.

There is a background to this pursuit of goals, and it is that if we do not act with commitment, we fall short, and then we find ourselves repeating cycles. What we are doing is trying to learn the same lesson. But when we learn the lessons, we move forward, we take leaps.

Rudd says that our commitment actually contains the seed of the goal, with the trust that we bring. Good fortune tends to follow. Things become clearer. It is our inner direction that becomes clearer, and it flows into the outer world.

At a higher level, which comes in its own time, there is devotion. This is an individual path, not a conventional, socially based path. What matters in life becomes an individual choice that we are responsible for, and our commitment has grown into love. And that love comes back to us from everywhere.

Ultimately, we accept that there is chaos at the heart of life, and it is only with open-hearted commitment that we can pass through the abyss, with trust. In this way we can participate in life's mystery. This is to say that in essence, life has a wildness about it; it is not a safe hiding hole. The hexagram of the Abyss (Water) is paired with hexagram 30, Radiance (Fire), for which the Siddhi is Rapture.

20 Hexagram 52: Mountain doubled

Another trigram is Mountain. Mountain is Gen, Keeping Still. Doubled, it is hexagram 52. I referred to Minford's commentary above.

Mountain means to stop, to cease motion, to be at rest. Mountain is strong; it is inner virtue. Nourish the noble spirit within you. Withdraw from the fray, the busy-ness of people, the entanglement in petty cares. At this time, know the truth that there is no fault in your being. Stillness prepares your mind to receive your next mission. Do not go beyond your duties at this time. This makes sense, because in one sense, a mountain is an obstruction, and two mountains, doubly so. It is appropriate to be still at this time. In stillness one cultivates energy; the self dissolves.

In Richard Rudd's account, the Mountain as shadow is the pressure of the world that all humans experience. It is the pressure of fear, and the fear that we are all isolated. Somehow, we must raise the frequency of the energy moving through us, then the way we experience life will change, as will the way we express ourselves.

The Mountain signifies rising above the stress. Perhaps we do this momentarily, but there is the possibility that we may do this permanently. Our problem is our tendency to see problems as something that can be solved by our cleverness. Rudd says the problem is, our solutions are actually rooted in the stress, and so the solutions will never free us from that stress. The gift offered is Restraint: learning the ability to stop reacting to fears. There are two types of reactions. Either we panic or we freeze; that is, we become frantic or depressed.

With restraint, we learn the stillness of the Mountain, and we learn to trust the rhythm of life. This gives us balance. Then we can serve more than ourselves. It can be difficult to slow down to the natural pace of life. One of the commentators tells the story of an enthusiastic farmer who wanted his corn to grow faster, so he went out to the field at night and pulled up each sprout a little higher, to give it a head start. The next day he was disappointed to find all the corn sprouts had wilted.

This is a childish story, but it probably describes us sometimes! We find it difficult to move at the pace of nature, and yet, at that pace, our actions become effortless. In this remaking of ourselves, we begin to focus more on intention. And our intention must be larger than ourselves; it must be for the good of all. And in doing so, we find that restraint begins to harness real power.

In Rudd's account, the end point is the very quality of Stillness. There is a state beyond the ordinary flurry of life, when the cycles have ended, having fulfilled themselves. As the Tao says, the beginning was stillness, and so too will be the end.

In the *Tao Te Ching*, stillness is the master of unrest. The things of nature are whole and full, and so the country is upright. The low is the foundation of the high. Stillness and tranquillity set things in order in the universe.

21 Hexagram 57: Wind doubled

Wind is another trigram, also designated as Wood. Doubled, it is 57, Xun. The Wind is conceived of as gentle. Wilhelm calls it Gentle Penetration. Huang calls it Proceeding Humbly. Although the wind is gentle, it is persistent, so it penetrates. It results in clarity of judgement that thwarts hidden motives. It is influence, such as a great personality that breaks up intrigues. It succeeds through what is small. It furthers to have somewhere to go.

Wind produces gradual effects through its persistence, not through violence. And its effects are enduring. It finds its way into every nook and cranny. It works always in the same direction, and it is clear about its goals. In this way the thoughts of a noble leader are assimilated by the people. The actions of such a leader are well-prepared.

Huang adds to this picture. He says that the persistence of the gentle wind means that it goes everywhere (proceeding humbly). In the same way, when Wood penetrates soil, it goes deeply, and it is easily accepted. The doubling of the same trigram indicates that the ruler repeats his order, and he carries out his command. In unstable situations, if a person is humble and gentle and is able to make friends with people, gaining their trust and support, he/she will eventually prevail.

There are two solid (yang) lines and a yielding line (yin) beneath them. And this image is doubled. It indicates that the person has patience and is willing to wait for the right time to accomplish an aim. The person must have the perspective of Confucius: at the outset, one's mind is in a state of equilibrium. During the vicissitudes of life, things may be turbulent; feelings are shaken up by ambitions and goals. But as things come to fulfilment, there is harmony. We must devote ourselves to moving between equilibrium and harmony. This is to proceed humbly.

The lines of this hexagram add nuances to this picture. For example, one should not be too retiring, because this would be to become weak and lose self-confidence.

Is the spirit of the Wind in the *Tao Te Ching*? In places, the suggestion is there. The Tao says, "Look, it cannot be seen – it is beyond form. Listen, it cannot be heard – it is beyond sound. Grasp, it cannot be held – it is intangible. Knowing the ancient beginning is the essence of Tao."

"Other people are contented, enjoying the sacrificial feast of the ox, but I alone am drifting, not knowing where I am, like the newborn babe before it learns to smile. I am alone without a place to go. Everyone is busy, but I alone am aimless. I am different. I am nourished by the Great Mother."

"High winds do not last all morning, heavy rain does not last all day. Why is this? If heaven and earth cannot make things eternal, how is it possible for people? He who follows the Tao is at one with the Tao. He who is virtuous experiences virtue."

"Man follows the earth. Earth follows heaven. Heaven follows the Tao. Tao follows what is natural."

"Counsel the ruler not to use force to conquer the universe, for this would only cause resistance. Force is followed by loss of strength. That is not the way of Tao."

"The softest thing in the universe overcomes the hardest thing in the universe. That which is without substance can enter where there is no room."

"The world is ruled by letting things take their course. It cannot be ruled by interfering."

"The stiff and unbending is the disciple of death. The gentle and yielding is the disciple of life. A tree that is unbending is easily broken. The harsh and strong will fall."

"The Tao of heaven is like the bending of a bow: the high is lowered and the low is raised. The Tao of heaven is to take from those who have too much and to give to those who do not have enough."

The trigram of Wind can be viewed through the perspective of Richard Rudd. He describes the Wind as Shadow first, then its appearance as a Gift, and lastly as a Siddhi – a state of bliss. The world that we live in has a shadow that is based on fear, from practical fears of personal safety to fears about food, sufficiency of money, and social safety. We share these fears with other people. The image of the Wind reminds us that this shadow is not within us; it is an aspect of the atmosphere we live in. That is a useful first step.

There is pressure to align ourselves with the atmosphere around us, and this has been individually reinforced through our history: our mother, our father, our family situation, and the beliefs and attitudes that dominated there. The atmosphere is characterised by unease, and our society ensures that this persists and is pervasive.

At a broader level, this is framed by our fears for our collective future. It is an extension of the fear of not knowing. And there is a socially prevalent response to this fear. It is the collective effort to deal with fears by seeking to create external security. And this effort seeks to create security with certainty. But certainty is an illusion.

However, the image of the wind has other aspects. We need to reframe our experience of the world: "Listen carefully to what comes on the wind." The effect of this gift is to enliven our intuition. Rudd's assertion is that this practice begins to heal us, and our frequency rises. We do this by embracing our experience and trusting in our safety, realising that there are many layers in our experience, and the intuition is in our body. He notes that indigenous people lived in their bodies, rather than always being absorbed by thoughts – the activity of the mind.

The elements of life are natural: sun, earth, water, wind, warmth, coolness, the aromas of flowers. Living an intellectual life, gradually we lose touch with those elements. This can include mindless social interaction, excessive consumption of television and other media: all the distractions in our lives. There are deeper issues in our lives that we need to reconnect with. Rudd's point is that life is ready to help us in this endeavour. The gift of intuition is life speaking to us. Listening to it, we grow in awareness. We also learn to trust more. Intuition is our body's system for interacting harmoniously with our environment.

The ways of our society are based on cleverness and force, seeking to conquer. The way of Tao is like the wind, a gentle and persistent force that aligns with nature. It embodies the movement that Confucius talked about: the movement from equilibrium to harmony. It follows a path that brings things to completion, that synthesises things. It seeks to integrate things.

It also dismantles the illusion that you are separate and alone. In this process, life becomes easier. Your body hums with life. Fear is gradually transcended. You feel part of life and can sense what is approaching, and feel part of that, too.

The I Ching speaks at the level of day-to-day life: the decisions we have to make and how to come to terms with our feelings. But it also speaks to something more, the deeper questions of our lives that may be difficult. It speaks to the central issue of ethics: will it be worthwhile for me to try to live in an ethical way?

Each of the trigrams examines a different aspect of life. But in the end, in any case, they are all aspects of the same life, and the answers are inter-related. Wind doubled brings clarity; this is the siddhi. Becoming more comfortable with our intuition, we learn the art of softness: the value of being gentle with life, and seeing what it reveals to you.

22 Hexagram 51: Thunder doubled

Thunder is another powerful natural image. Doubled, it is 51, Zhen, Arousing. It stands for movement. Alfred Huang calls it "Taking Action". It signifies things coming back to life in spring. It is also the first son, who seizes rule with energy and power. A single yang line enters at the bottom and pushes upward, challenging the two yin lines. Just so, thunder bursts forth from the earth and shakes all around. It is also called Quake. It terrifies, but then, lo!, people break out into laughter, with joy and merriment.

And the sage does not let fall the sacrificial spoon and chalice. He examines himself and sets his life in order.

Does the *Tao Te Ching* refer to Thunder? In a way, it does: "The space between heaven and earth is like bellows and pipes, empty yet inexhaustible, producing more with movement."

Some of its allusions to thunder are wide-sweeping: "Carrying vitality and consciousness, embracing them as one, can you keep them from parting?" [10]

The Tao is interested in what is alarming. People are swayed by favour and disgrace. "Why does high status greatly affect our person? The reason we have a lot of trouble is that we have selves. If we had no selves, what troubles would we have?" [13]

Richard Rudd considers the three faces of Thunder: Agitation, Initiative and Awakening. The shadow is the feeling of agitation because we do not control our world. Often, events seem random as well. It creates an atmosphere of low trust as a constant state. When shocks come, they challenge us, because they threaten our sense of security. At a deeper level, shocks suggest the ultimate shock to come: death.

The ordinary human answer to this predicament is to become competitive. By winning, and also, by beating others, we experience victories that make us feel better, at least, temporarily. It can lead to wild acts, or to deep states of depression.

The second face of this hexagram is Initiative. Here, competitiveness is exchanged for creativity. To do this, one has to turn one's back on conventionality and learn to live independently. Thus, one will find one's own initiative. This is actually a leap into the higher self. We harness our difference and our excellence. This will stir powerful responses: what we have described as Thunder. But the force of thunder is a force of life; it awakens life, and it will support you.

Note, this is not about being a leader of people, but about being an initiator. It can be powerful enough to affect the collective consciousness. The essence of Thunder is Awakening; it breaks through the state of sleep to make new things possible. It is a way of seeing that sees through everything. And Rudd says the energy of Awakening is love.

This is a shocking message. We might be more comfortable thinking that we are trying to understand life, and we are trying to do the ethical thing in life, when this message is beyond that manageable pathway. But Rudd puts it simply: there are only two states; either you are asleep or you are awake. He says that this Siddhi is the ground on which all the other siddhis are founded.

23 Hexagram 30: Fire doubled

Fire is associated with light and warmth. It is variously called Brightness, Brilliance, Radiance. The trigram consists of a solid line at top and bottom, and a broken line in the middle. It is as if the dark line is clinging to something, as flames cling to wood. As water pours down from heaven, so fire flames up from the earth. Fire stands for the radiance of nature. It can also stand for the sun. (Conversely, Water can stand for the moon.)

The doubled trigram is 30, showing Brightness doubled. The concept of perseverance is an aspect of Fire, because the luminous object is giving out light, and it must have perseverance within. As with all the trigrams, Fire has moral lessons for us. The dedicated person clings to right, and thereby they can shape the world. Wilhelm says human life on earth is conditioned and unfree, but when we recognise this and make ourselves dependent on the natural forces of the cosmos, we acquire clarity. Some commentators call it Supreme Intelligence because it brings to light all you need to know.

Slowly, trigram by trigram and hexagram by hexagram, the I Ching builds up a picture of a worthwhile, and joyful, way to live life. Wilhelm goes on to say, "In the image of Fire, the great person, by perpetuating brightness, illuminates the four corners of the world." The hexagram Water doubled displays the way to deal with a difficult or dangerous situation. The hexagram Fire doubled displays how to distinguish between right and wrong – clarity. One's attitude must be sincere and whole-hearted.

The *Tao Te Ching* is aware of light and its qualities, and its power as a metaphor. It says, "The wise student hears of the Tao and practises it diligently. The average student hears of the Tao and gives it thought now and then. The foolish student hears of the Tao and laughs aloud. Hence it is said, 'The bright path seems dim.'"

Elsewhere it says, "Using the outer light, return to insight, and in this way, be saved from harm. This is to learn constancy."

Richard Rudd sees this hexagram in terms of desire. Desire is an inherent quality of humans, a natural hunger. Desire urges us forward, it entices us towards achievement. But, being imperfect, we make mistakes. However, we have the capacity to learn from our mistakes. Desire inspires us to want to experience everything.

In Buddhism, desire is the cause of all suffering. It ensues from that sense of yearning or longing that we have. Then we either seek to fulfil the desire or to escape from it. And desire operates in cycles; it creates patterns in us. The object in Buddhism is to reject desire, to be desireless. The message in Richard Rudd's work is not that. He urges us to accept desire as an essential aspect of life. But desire presents us with a paradox.

The paradox is that the healthiest way to live is to embrace desire, but to embrace it lightly. The hexagram 30 is paired with 29: Water doubled. The gift of 29 is whole-heartedness. The gift of 30 is lightness. As an instruction, it is: "Lighten up". The effect of this attitude is that we enter into life more deeply rather than less so. It is to expand our consciousness, and not to behave as a victim of life.

In one of his movies, Billie Conolly (the Scottish comedian) makes the statement: "It is all ridiculous," and in the movie he is a man who is living lightly but deeply, and fearlessly. One knows that the essence of life cannot be harmed. Gradually, one can let go of suffering.

Rudd also talks about the siddhi for this gene key. It is Rapture. From the thwarted state in which we begin, pervaded by desires we cannot control or even manage well, we evolve to a state of rapture. When we lighten up, remembering that "it is all ridiculous", we are open to rapture. It is to dissolve into the fire, the celestial fire. As Rudd expresses it: "This is to *be* one's longing".

Rudd paints extraordinary pathways for living. The I Ching moves from being a tool for divination to being a book of wisdom and now, a manual for spiritual evolution.

24 Hexagram 58: Lake doubled

This hexagram: 58, Dui, is made up of Lake doubled: Lake upon Lake. The trigram Lake is two yang lines with one yin line on top. It stands for the third (or youngest) daughter. Wilhelm says it is called the Joyous. It is the yielding quality of the top line that accounts for the joy present here, because it is supported by two strong lines. There is firmness and strength within.

The Lake manifests itself outwardly as gentle. The joyous mood is infectious, and therefore it brings success. Humans are wont to use force to achieve their ends, but force does not give rise to willingness. On the other hand, where people are won by friendliness, they are willing to take on burdens and hardships in order to achieve a common end. Such is the power of joy.

Two lakes replenish one another, making their benefit abundant. In the field of human knowledge, it becomes a refreshing and revitalising force, when people meet to discuss and cultivate knowledge with goodwill. This is preferable to where people pursue their knowledge individually and do not explore its application for social good. This is Wilhelm's commentary.

How does Wilhelm's view compare with Alfred Huang's? One of the interesting aspects of Huang is that he comments on the sequence of the hexagrams. In the I Ching, Dui is 58. Before it comes 57: Wind doubled, which Huang calls "Proceeding Humbly". This explains why people feel joyous. When they proceed humbly together, joy is possible.

Huang says "Joy is favourable to being steadfast and upright. It is acting in accord with the will of heaven and in correspondence with the wishes of the people. How great is the power of giving people joyfulness! It stimulates them to do everything possible."

Does the *Tao Te Ching* have anything to say about the lake? No, but one can understand why. In the Tao, there are streams. The streams flow into rivers, and the rivers flow into the seas. There is a message about the Tao in this: the seas, being below the rivers, receive them all. The sea does not see itself as being superior, so it does not place itself above the rivers. Just so, the Tao is humble and therefore lasts eternally.

The lake sits outside this framework, as it is a still body of water. That stillness ought to remind us of the thinking of Confucius: we begin in equilibrium, we persevere through trials and achieve goals, and our end-state is harmony. The lake is the expression of that stillness and joy.

The Tao also has something to say about joy: "When the people follow the Tao, they are content for their lives to be simple. Their food is plain and good, their clothes fine and simple, their homes are secure; they are happy in their ways."

Richard Rudd says that the shadow side of gene key 58 is Dissatisfaction. It is partnered with 52: Stress. It is a general restlessness rather than a specific emotion like sadness or anger. It is an aspect of modern life. In our society there are even forces that cultivate this restlessness, in order to sell some kind of "satisfactions", generally ones that create dependencies (addictions). The larger implication of this problem is that it teaches us to seek the resolution of our dissatisfactions in outer sources rather than internally.

Rudd extends this thought to say that the root of our dissatisfaction is that we look to its resolution in the future. And thinking is part of this. That is a sentiment that is expressed in many spiritual contexts: books, groups, religions. However, it is difficult to see how to use this knowledge. It doesn't seem possible to get through life functionally if we don't think at all! And confronting the problem directly is subject to defeat.

Rudd also points out a great irony: the presence of this dissatisfaction in society drives people to improve things! But it does not solve the broader problem of the ongoing reality of dissatisfaction. Moreover, the shadows of the 58th and 52nd gene keys reinforce each other, and collectively, the shadow deepens.

The waters of the lake are stirred up. However, the path changes when we accept that there is no future state of perfection in the external world. We must turn inwards. But then we discover that we cannot produce our own happiness either. But this quest is wrapped in a paradox: we don't need to create happiness; it already exists. The Gift inside us is Vitality.

The point is that this is our natural state. Life expresses itself through us without resistance. The lake is full. This brings us near to other people, because life always seeks itself, and it seeks itself through other people. Joy unites people as they work towards higher goals. This is Vitality. We might say we feel invigorated. This is freedom for joy.

There is an improvement in social skills as well, because our empathy to understand others increases, and we can work with other people more in line with natural forces rather than interfering. Rudd says the 58th Gift is irrepressible. He is prone to bold statements, but this is what one might think of joyousness! He says, we learn to move in deep harmony with our environment, in service to the common benefit.

So, one answer to the question of how to loosen our grasp on our desire for a better future is to awaken ourselves to the vitality of the present. Dissatisfaction is being transformed into vitality. At the same time, this vitality is loosened from our individual self; life is larger. Then our awareness can stretch into infinity. And bliss occurs, as a byproduct. Life wells up continually in us.

This is Rudd's outline of what is possible for humans. He talks about enlightenment, and that it is not something we can precipitate. But we can work with the Gifts and deliver ourselves from the Shadows which precipitate the unfavourable attitudes and actions that invite misfortune.

25 Hexagram 1: Heaven doubled

Hexagram 1 in the I Ching is made up of the trigram Heaven doubled: six unbroken yang lines. This stands for the primal power of the universe. It is light-giving, active, strong, and of the spirit. Its essence is power or energy unrestrained, and time. Thus, its qualities include the persistence of things in time, or duration.

The image of the hexagram is Heaven. It is the power that acts on the universe, and the power that acts in the world of humans, so it is called the Creative, Qian. Wilhelm says, "The Creative works sublime success, furthering through perseverance." It has the four attributes of *yuan, heng, li, zhen*. *Yuan* means sublime and initiating; *heng* means prosperous and smooth; *li* means favourable and beneficial; and *zhen* means steadfast and upright. These four attributes are sprinkled through the I Ching. A few of the hexagrams have all four attributes.

These attributes express the philosophical aspects of the I Ching, which explain the relationships between Heaven, Earth and humans, that is, how humans can live naturally in the world, following the natural order. The four attributes likewise stand for the four stages of development or growth.

The Heaven trigram doubled recognises the fundamental law of the universe: change. Huang says, "The way of Initiating (the Creative) is change and transformation, so that each being obtains its true nature and destiny and the union of great harmony is preserved. This is what is favourable and upright. The Initiating is high above all beings and thus all countries are united in peace."

Heaven's movement is constant, persistent and stable. It follows its orbit without deviation, thus maintaining the equilibrium. It acts without ceasing, and all our actions should be in accord with the proper time and circumstances. When the time or circumstances are not suitable, one should forebear and have patience. The omen animal for this hexagram is the dragon. This mythical animal was revered in ancient China.

Confucius said that the first and second hexagrams are a pair: "Creative (Heaven) and Receptive (Earth) are the foundation of the I Ching", and they are essential for understanding it. They exist without beginning or end, and they introduce the cycles of nature. They teach us that we should move in tune with the seasons. There is a time to advance and a time to be still. There are lessons in all the variations of nature. It constitutes a moral foundation as much as a natural foundation. For example, one should accept good fortune without lapsing into arrogance.

But the Creative also refers to development at the individual level. Wilhelm says, "the superior man makes himself strong and untiring." To know the Heaven hexagram is to know Heaven as an inspiring force. One's response is to make an offering, and so, one will succeed. There may be obstacles on your way, but you should not be dismayed.

In the *Tao Te Ching*, Tao is the originator of Heaven and Earth. "Heaven is eternal and Earth is everlasting. The reason they can be eternal and everlasting is that they do not favour themselves; they put themselves last."

"When one's work is done and one's name is becoming distinguished, to withdraw into obscurity is the way of heaven."

"Humanity takes its law from the earth; the earth takes its law from heaven; heaven takes its law from the Tao. Tao follows what is natural."

"Without going outside, you may know the whole world. Without looking through the window, you may know the ways of heaven. The farther you go, the less you know. Thus the sage knows without travelling; he sees without looking; he works without doing."

"The Tao of heaven does not strive, and yet it overcomes. It does not speak, and yet it is answered. It does not ask, and yet is supplied with all its needs."

"The Tao of heaven is to take from those who have too much and give to those who do not have enough. Man's way is different. He takes from those who do not have enough to give to those who already have too much."

"The Tao of heaven is impartial. Sages keep their faith and do not pressure others."

Richard Rudd's book also begins with Heaven doubled. In the Gene Keys it is called "From Entropy to Syntropy". Rudd says the four hexagrams: 1, 2, 63 and 64, contain four essential principles for life. As with all the gene keys, 1 starts with the Shadow, which here is Entropy. That is followed by the Gift of Freshness, and the Siddhi of Beauty. Once again, this is a strange concatenation of concepts.

Rudd starts with Entropy: energy in the universe appears to be moving from order to chaos. This is humanity's biggest problem. It is experienced as feelings of numbness and gloominess, and to that extent, energy is unavailable for doing work. And humans largely deny this state. Being emotional, it comes in waves, and it comes unpredictably. It generates longing and melancholy.

Entropy keeps the planet in a low level of frequency. Awareness is about accepting the energy latent in the shadow; it is a fertile state. Entropy and creativity are in a dance with each other. Trying to fix the melancholy (as we generally seek to do) stops it from completing itself. Out of the darkness comes light and joy that we feel the urge to express. Thus the gift is called Freshness. It burns with an inner fire, as if it came from another world.

This gift will emerge naturally, but it cannot be forced. Creativity requires us to be patient, attentive, and ready to be alone with ourselves at times. Our task is simply to allow evolution to move through us, towards a permanent state of love, beauty and unity.

At the Siddhi level, light is all that exists, and it shines through human awareness as Beauty. True beauty is unity, which is also emptiness. The notion of syntropy is that all that exists is the movement of energy within infinite dimensions. All there is is consciousness and love.

26 Hexagram 2: Earth doubled

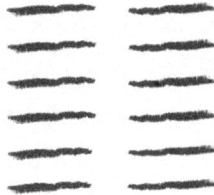

This hexagram is made up of broken lines only. The three broken lines of the trigram represent Earth. It is darkness, the yielding, the receptive and nurturing power of yin (female). Earth doubled is the complement to hexagram 1. The first and second hexagrams are not combatants; they are complementary. They complete each other. Hexagram 2 represents nature in contrast to spirit. It is earth in contrast to heaven; it is space rather than time, female rather than male. In the individual, it is the senses rather than the spiritual.

Wilhelm calls hexagram 2 the Receptive. There is a hierarchy here, because the Receptive must be activated by the Creative. Where the Receptive (earth) seeks to operate apart from the Creative (heaven), evil occurs. When people try to dominate, they go astray. Just as with hexagram 1, this hexagram has the four attributes of *yuan, heng, li, zhen*. It emphasises the centrality of these qualities to admirable conduct or to an admirable character: sublime and initiating (*yuan*); prosperous and smooth (*heng*); favourable and beneficial (*li*); and steadfast and upright (*zhen*).

The hexagram concerns potential coming into being, and it is associated with the perseverance of a mare. The horse belongs to the earth and is strong and swift, and as a mare it is gentle and devoted. It does not take the lead, but lets itself be guided. It learns from the situation what is required. It is adept at gaining the cooperation of others. The earth is able to carry all things without distinction. It is able to bear with people and things.

Huang calls hexagram 2 Responding. He says humans have to be responsive to heaven's will. The six yin lines denote the most responsive, flexible, devoted and humble qualities. Together, heaven and earth create the conditions for life: "After heaven and earth have come into existence, myriad beings are produced." Creative bestows the seeds, and the Receptive brings them to life.

Huang also discusses the way that hexagram 2 indicates we should live. The quality of responsiveness is that we are responsive to the present conditions of the situation. We do not live in a predetermined way: formulaic, programmed. We are alive to the present. Kun is always in touch with the earth, with its boundlessness, resting in steadfastness.

Hexagram 1 is the most yang; hexagram 2 is the most yin. The entire I Ching is based on the interplay between these two forms of energy. It is the interplay between hard and soft, strong and flexible, firm and gentle. Huang says, "Yin is the most gentle and submissive; when put in motion it is strong and firm."

One would expect the *Tao Te Ching* to say something about the place of earth in its understanding of the universe. The universe begins with non-being: "Non-being is called the beginning of heaven and earth; being is called the mother of all things. Heaven is eternal, Earth is everlasting. Was it not by their very selflessness that they managed to fulfil themselves?"

The Tao is the spirit of all things, vast, beyond individual identities and self-importance. It enables this endlessness. "Heaven and Earth do not act from (the impulse of) any wish to be benevolent."

The beginning is wholeness or unity. The Tao says, "When unity was obtained of old, Heaven became clear by attaining unity, Earth became steady by attaining unity, spirit was quickened by attaining unity, valley streams were filled by attaining unity; all beings were born by attaining unity, and by attaining unity, lords acted rightly for the sake of the world."

We must remember the vision of Confucius, of life beginning in equilibrium, expending itself in activity, and working back towards harmony. The Tao says, "The space between Heaven and Earth is like a bellows and pipes, empty yet inexhaustible."

Richard Rudd sees hexagram 2 in terms of the narrative of the universe. He calls it: "Returning to the One". Whereas hexagram 1 is about energy and light, hexagram 2 is about the darkness that receives the light. It is about space and form. Even at the shadow level there is the message that life has purpose. The great motherly embrace pulls us all into a single unity. Your personal resonance with the great truth of unity determines the frequency of light that passes through you. It indicates the place we occupy in our evolutionary journey.

The shadow is called Dislocation. It means the perception that you are lost in space/time. Our evolutionary journey began with the acquisition of instinct. Gradually we acquired the power of thought as our brains developed. Rudd says that at this point in our history, we are poised for a leap into awareness that is centred in our solar plexus, and it will reawaken the sense of unity.

However, in our modern society we have taken the path of technology, a massive technological revolution that has distanced us from nature. It is inhibiting our instinctive awareness. It is associated with our collective fear that we will destroy ourselves. We feel separate from nature. So, our pattern of life is conflicted.

The hopeful sign is that we are witnesses to our situation. We can see our dilemma. We cannot change it, but we do not need to. Here, Rudd offers a powerful observation: in the early days of the I Ching, hexagram 2 may not have been the second hexagram; it may have been the first! Mythically it makes more sense, to start with the female. To put the male first makes force the dominant quality rather than nurturing and trust.

The name in the I Ching, Kun, means Field, and to move in harmony with the field. In Rudd's work, the Gift is Orientation. There is a shift, perhaps precipitated by an event or a crisis. You change your orientation to life. There is an increased sense of synchronicity, which is to say, you see your life in a broader context. There is a rhythm in life. You could say, it is more magical.

Along with synchronicity, we develop the feeling that we are connected; we are not isolated. We are part of the unity, as the *Tao Te Ching* notes. The larger agenda of life is to bring all beings into an awareness of their unity. In fact, the Siddhi for this gene key is Unity. It is the divine feminine. It is enlightenment.

Rudd says, the Siddhi is the original nature of consciousness itself, and it manifests in a beautiful plan unfolding in space and time, swept along by evolution. Our goal is to realise our unity.

27 Returning to medical matters

I mentioned earlier the small matter of my having probably had a minor stroke. There is evidence in my brain, bleeding evident in the MRI scan. But I have no detectable impairments. The doctors are concerned, and they are collecting data. I am not allowed to drive a car for four weeks. I have slowed down my work, but I continue.

The next thing to do (in my dislocated journey) was to describe the eight trigrams and their meanings, their occurrence in the *Tao Te Ching*, and the treatment that Richard Rudd gives the eight doubled trigrams. I have done that now.

There is no forward path yet in the medical realm. There is the addition of a few tablets, which is simply a small addition to my daily routines. I am doing more walking, because I cannot drive the car. I think about the state of my mind; I observe my body a little more constantly, but all is functioning well. I continue my daily yoga routines, and I do a yoga class twice a week.

I am in regular conversation with a few people who are concerned about my welfare.

There is, despite all this, a detriment to the eyesight in my right eye. The visual field is fuzzy in the centre. The peripheral vision is fine, but the centre is distorted. The eye doctor said it is macular degeneration. In my mid-seventies, do I have to start thinking of myself as growing old?

Not just growing old, but deteriorating? I accept the verdict of chronology. There is no escaping the fact that I was born in 1950, but I have withdrawn my allegiance from the dictum that life is inherently entropic. I note that Richard Rudd's description of Heaven doubled (see above) starts with the idea of entropy, but this is the shadow; it is not the essence.

So, day by day, I am wondering about this medical episode and what I might be able to do to respond to it intelligently, with spirit. I don't need a definite conclusion about what the medical episode was, so I am not greatly invested in that. I am interested in the experience I had, and I am interested in the ongoing detriment to my eyesight. I am interested in what I might be able to learn to help myself.

The other day I had a remarkable reading of the I Ching. I got 2: Receptive, changing to 12: Stagnation.

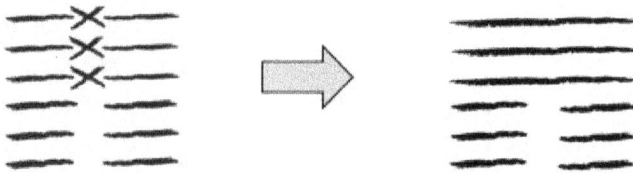

2: Receptive: Kun   12: Stagnation: Pi

Hexagram 2, as we saw earlier, consists of six broken lines. But to change to 12, the upper three lines have to change to yang (unbroken). In all the years I have been throwing the I Ching coins, I don't think this has ever happened. In 12, Heaven is above Earth. This situation is worth examining, because the relation of the two trigrams to each other in a hexagram makes a great deal of difference to the meaning.

When Earth is above Heaven, the hexagram is 11: Peace: Tai. But when Heaven is above Earth, we get 12: Stagnation: Pi. 11 seems auspicious, but 12 seems ominous or foreboding. Why is this?

The answer is that some trigrams tend to move upwards and some tend to move downwards. Heaven tends to move up, while Earth tends to move down, so in 12, Heaven and Earth are moving away from each other. They are not communicating, so it is not a good situation. In hexagram 11, that is not so; Heaven and Earth are

96

moving towards each other and are in communion. There is a flow of energy that can help to bring things to maturity.

In contrast, in 12, the communication is blocked, and it is not a good time to try to complete projects. Heaven and Earth create the conditions for life, but if they in the wrong relation to each other, there is obstruction. The I Ching is based on the interplay between hard and soft, strong and flexible, firm and gentle. Here, heaven and earth are turned away from each other. It is as if inferior people have come into positions of power and are standing in the way of wiser people.

These two hexagrams are in a special relationship to each other. In fact, in this instance that is true twice over. Hexagrams 11 and 12 are opposites, meaning that when each line turns into its opposite, one hexagram turns into the other. But, they are also inverse hexagrams: when the whole hexagram rotates about itself, you get the other hexagram.

So, there is a whole world involved in the relationships of the hexagrams with each other. Looking at 11 and 12 is just a glimpse. This emphasises that the fundamental theme of the I Ching is change. All is change and evolution.

The advice of hexagram 12 is to focus on the ordinary things of life rather than seeking public prominence and honours. Focus on virtue to cast out hardship. Work through the receptive and the power of earth.

What do I take from this? I think I need to focus on what my body is saying, to pay attention to that rather than on goals in the big world. This is to say, I should increase my awareness of my body and emotions, from moment to moment. There are things I think I need to learn, about what my body is doing and how I could play an active part in its healing. The fact that the first hexagram was 2: Receptive, emphasises this focus on the physical body. Then the fact that it turns to 12: Stagnation (or Obstruction) indicates to me that there has been a crisis, and the current situation needs remedying.

"Work through the receptive and the power of earth" shows that there is an active role for me. I am not a helpless victim of a situation. There is something I can do. Noting what Richard Rudd says, we are poised for a leap into awareness that is centred in our solar plexus, which is to say we are called to be more attentive to our feelings. The Gift of 2 is Orientation: you change your orientation to life. There is an increased sense of synchronicity and connection with others. Hexagram 2 is connected with the original nature of consciousness itself.

28 A response to the medical episode

A few months ago I bought a book at a book fair called *The Brain's Way of Healing* by Norman Doidge. I thought it was an interesting topic, and I thought I might read it sometime. There are many books of that kind in my library, and that is fine. But a couple of weeks ago I noticed it, and suddenly it was much more relevant. So, I started reading it, and it was full of stories of people who had had severe medical problems involving the brain, and who had the idea that they could work with their own brain to try to improve their physical condition.

I don't usually read medical books. We all have our specialties, but medicine is not one of mine. But I was interested in the idea of the brain being able to help us to heal, and us being able to work with the brain to facilitate that process. I happen to have many books about the relationship between the brain, the mind, and healing. It is a field of thought that is now ripe for my investigation.

As if to reinforce this idea, the I Ching gave me the hexagram 50: Cauldron: Ding. The image goes a long way back into Chinese history, to the Xia dynasty, then the Shang, and the Zhou dynasties, when a new bronze cauldron was cast for the beginning of each dynasty (and often, not just one but nine bronze cauldrons). Inscribed on it/them were omen animals and the constitution of the new regime. Accordingly, 50 may stand for the establishment of a new regime, not simply politically, but also personally. What new regime is required for me – new ideas, new practices?

If we think of hexagram 50 as being part of a pair, the pair is 49 and 50, and 49 stands for abolishing the old. The Cauldron in 50 symbolises cooking food and offering it to the ancestors in order to nourish the new regime. The trigrams are Wood below Fire, so they symbolise cooking. The commentary says this is a time of supreme good fortune. It is prosperous and smooth.

There is more. There were two moving lines, which changes the hexagram to 28: Great Exceeding.

50: Cauldron: Ding   28: Great Exceeding: Da Guo

This seems foreboding, but also appropriate. Didn't the incident that occurred indicate an excess of pressure, causing the bleed in my brain? The image of 28 is the ridgepole of a house which is loaded to excess and the two ends of it are weak, so the ridgepole is in danger of collapsing. However, the commentary does not foretell doom. Instead, it suggests what needs to happen.

It is a time when extraordinary action is needed. It is time to go somewhere or do something to remedy the situation. If you look at the trigrams, Wind is below Lake. Wind is smooth movement and

Lake is joy, so overall it is favourable. One may stand alone without fear, and withdraw from the world without regret. The message is that one should not play the part of victim, but take action to remedy the situation.

To apply this message, I continue to read the book on the brain. I continue to do daily yoga sessions and meditate. I walk. I eat good food. I take on board the stories in the book, always thinking about what relates to my situation and what I might adapt to myself. I remind myself: extraordinary action is needed, but the path is smooth, and it is a time of good fortune.

I could also say that the reference to the ridgepole of the house is a reference to the roof, the top of the house. It is a parallel to the notion that the issue is about the head of a person, the brain – the top. These meanings flow naturally when one uses the I Ching regularly.

29 The I Ching's story continues

I go day by day. There are no instant solutions. Is there any change at all? This is a strange space. In the brain book, I am reading about people who have had strokes, and they have serious problems: they can't speak, they can't think clearly, they can't keep their balance. I am free of all those impairments. But I have the problem with my right eye, and reading is more difficult. And often, a headache seems to hover near me, and what does that mean? Is it an(other) imminent stroke? Is it a sign of other serious trouble approaching?

(The eye doctor says the problem with my right eye has nothing to do with the stroke. I say, the first time I noticed the problem with my right eye was after the day I had the headache. He would argue that that is the fallacy of "*post hoc ergo propter hoc*": "after the fact, therefore, because of the fact". I know the rule; I learned it in high school. But the association is there for me. My experience was, I had a headache, and then I discovered a problem with my eye.)

When the headache hovers, I give it my attention. I stop what I am doing. I endeavour to relax and breathe. It fades away. I go back to work. I know there are people who say I should put the work away altogether. Do something else entirely, like gardening. But the story is here; it is me living. I am myself; I am not the gardener. And in the I Ching, the story goes on, it keeps evolving. It never gets stuck in one place.

This morning, I got two hexagrams: 18 and 31. 18 is "Work on what has been spoiled". Rather obvious, I thought. How often has this hexagram come up for me? With no moving lines, five times over the last four years, which is to say, quite a lot (considering that there are sixty-four hexagrams). The other hexagram, 31, is "Mutual Influence". How often has this hexagram occurred for me? With no moving lines, never, not at all; bearing in mind that there are only a couple of hexagrams out of the sixty-four that have not occurred for me yet. But it comes up now. Surely that is interesting?

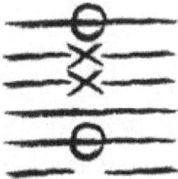

18: Work on what has been spoiled: Gu

31: Mutual Influence: Xian

Another name used by commentators for 18 is "Correcting the Corruption". The trigrams are Wind below Mountain. It can be visualised as the wind blowing around at the foot of the mountain, amidst the undergrowth. But it is dense, so the wind cannot penetrate. It means that the air there is stale, and things decay. It is a good image for corruption.

The good that the solidity of the mountain usually offers is now fostering decay, because the wind needs to penetrate, to blow freshness into the space, and it cannot. There is another ancient image that is even stronger. It is of a bowl in which five poisonous creatures are put: a snake, a scorpion, a centipede, a gecko and a toad – until one of them has killed and eaten the others. This became a venom which was capable of crazing and killing a victim.

It refers to a time when people have forgotten to be steadfast and upright. It is also an assertion that the corruption can be conquered now if we take action. We all carry within us burdens and scars from our past, going all the way back to the view of the world we received from our parents. These are the things we need to overcome, finding new ways.

I learn this: the problem has surfaced now because I am able to address it now, and the tools will be given to me to do so. I must forge a new way. The commentators express it in different ways, but the essence is: this is a beneficial time to engage in an adventurous project. Prepare carefully, and afterwards, inspect thoroughly. It is a time of renovation. What is it that needs to be renewed?

What of 31: Mutual Influence? As said, this is a hexagram I receive only rarely. The trigrams are Mountain and Lake, and the mountain is below the lake. How does the I Ching interpret this? The mountain below provides a foundation for the lake, while the water in the lake provides moisture for the mountain. There is a mutual attraction between them. They move naturally towards each other. In the sequence of the I Ching, it stands for the attraction between a young man and a young woman, and the hexagram that follows is 32: Duration, which stands for marriage.

While the hexagram deals with the affection of courtship, it extends to the broader theme of universal love, of seeing the loving connection between all things (unity). Hua-Ching Ni gives a helpful comment about this: "When one becomes empty, one becomes receptive to positive energy, to love." The negative influences that one should reject are restlessness and impulsiveness. The name of the hexagram, Xian, means "to touch the heart".

All that I have to do is to do today as well as I can. The paradox is that the best way to do this is to work and relax, and not worry, and to notice and enjoy what the day brings. Hexagram 31 has the firmness and strength of the mountain, along with the gentleness and joyfulness of the lake.

30 An experience of being an I Ching adept

I have attended the Woodford Folk Festival in Queensland many times. It is six days, from Christmas to New Year. One year, I had struck up a conversation with a stranger when, having heard that I studied the I Ching, she urged me to do a reading for her. I initially resisted, because I had no materials with me – no I Ching book, no coins, no cloth on which to throw the coins…. All the necessary paraphernalia. But she was insistent, and I ended up doing it. So, for that time I was, publicly, an I Ching adept.

Later, I gave an account of the encounter in one of my books: *Long Time Approaching: An Incomplete Memoir* (Chapter 73). Here it is, below.

An I Ching reading at the Woodford Folk Festival

At Woodford, you could meet someone on a pathway somewhere in the valley, between one music tent and another, and simply start talking with each other. Or you might be sitting on a hillside and someone would come up to you. And instantly you would be talking about something deeply. Connections were easily made.

One time I was sitting on the hillside near a perplexing bamboo sculpture and a lady walked up. She asked me if it was okay to sit down, and it was. Soon we were talking about the I Ching. Then she said, "Do the I Ching for me." I said, "I can't. I don't have anything with me: no coins, no book."

She didn't think that was a sufficient excuse. I tried again: "I don't have the coins with me." She countered with, "We can just use ordinary coins." I continued to resist: "Ordinary coins are money. It's not appropriate."

"Yes, but the Chinese coins were money too. We can just use ordinary coins."

I was losing. But I couldn't do it. "Listen," I said, "there are sixty-four hexagrams. I don't remember all of them. You could throw a hexagram and then I wouldn't be able to interpret it for you." That's a rather solid argument.

Her answer was, "I'm sure you'll be okay. Let's just do it."

It's laughable, isn't it? There is no common sense at Woodford. Her faith in me seemed to require my faith in the universe. We proceeded.

We found three coins of the same size, decided which side was yin and which was yang, and she formulated her question. I said, "Don't tell me the question. Then I can be free with what I say about the hexagram, and you can tell me if it makes sense to you."

I took out some paper and a pen, and we made a space where she could throw the coins. I drew the six lines as she threw them. I forget whether there were any moving lines (which means a second hexagram is involved), but in any case, I looked at the two trigrams and as it happened, I knew which hexagram it was. I understand the dynamics between the trigrams and I gave my interpretation of the hexagram for her.

I asked her if it made sense, and she looked pensive. She said that what I said was very relevant to her situation, and helpful. We hugged.

31 Addressing scepticism

Doing the I Ching for a stranger was definitely okay at Woodford. The atmosphere is open and accommodating. There is scope for friendly and profitable encounters. But in the outside world it is frequently not so. We live in a rationalistic world where any systems of thought that have randomness as a central principle are scorned. And the scorn is vitriolic: "Rubbish! Ridiculous!"

One goes through various responses to such sentiments. One can try to devise convincing arguments. One can appeal to respected people who have used the I Ching, for example. It is often said that the main reason Richard Wilhelm's edition became so popular in the West was because the Foreword was written by Carl Jung, the Swiss psychologist.

One can talk about the I Ching as a body of work and point to its extraordinary internal coherence, its flawless structure based on the binary system (throwing the coins six times, disregarding moving lines for now, gives us $2^6 = 64$). One can point to its use over an extraordinarily long period of time. There are arguments like that, many of them.

Sometimes friends will put the question to you, as if to say, I don't doubt it myself, but what would you say to a sceptic? They are looking for the assurance you can give them. It is expected that you will have the arguments ready.

I mentioned this issue in a book I wrote many years ago. This was my statement then, in *To the Bush and Back to Business*:

"There was never any question in my mind that immersing myself in the I Ching and seeking to live out of its conception of the world, its cosmic perspective, was a worthwhile enterprise. I only raise this because when I've confessed my predilection for the I Ching, some people have said, 'Oh, yes, I remember dabbling with that in the early 1970s. It was quite fashionable for a time. But I could never make much sense of it. And you're still using it?' (With the inference, why? You didn't grow up?)"

Being "grown up", or rational, or realistic, are camouflage words. Mostly they simply mean we have opted into conventional ways of seeing the world. We no longer question life. We are no longer looking deeply into life. It is not that we should be looking for "answers" (just as dangerous as not asking the questions at all), but we could be looking for life to make sense in an unfolding way.

If you are looking for life to make sense, then there are many things to notice and respond to, every day. Today it makes sense that the I Ching should tell me to observe what may have led to a "minor stroke" and address it. What is the "corruption" that I can correct in myself? How does one become empty, and open to the positive energy that is about?

I remember that much of the criticism is about rational things, not meaning or significance. The critics are wanting to hear something specific: they will get a letter in seven days, and it will offer them a highly rewarding position that they have coveted. That is not what the I Ching offers. What it will offer is a context in which to see your life constructively. It is a moral perspective. It is a developmental viewpoint. It won't help you to conquer the world, but it may lead you into peace and wisdom.

Carl Jung, in his memorial address for Richard Wilhelm, said. "People have become weary of scientific specialisation and rationalistic intellectualism. They want to hear truths which broaden rather than restrict them, which do not obscure but enlighten, which do not run off them like water, but penetrate them to the marrow."

And as Forest Gump periodically said, "And that's all I've got to say about that!"

32 Facing paradox

There are people who have an easy flow of truisms. There is often only a slim difference between essential truths and glib platitudes. One must be fierce, but not too fierce, to make the correct distinctions. This is the challenge of recognising and facing paradox.

When you throw the coins of the I Ching and receive a hexagram (or two), you are subject to the way in which your situation has been defined. The translator (or commentator) uses certain words and phrases, and draws on certain sets of meaning, which could be psychological, historical, mythological, cultural or some mix of these concepts and information. This will make a difference to the messages you receive from the reading.

I have reached the stage where choosing which book to consult is an important part of my routine, as important as the way I set up my space in preparation, the way I prepare my mind, the question I ask (or don't ask), the way in which I throw the coins, or the notebook I use to record the lines. Each writer offers a different perspective and emphasises different things. It means that you think about different aspects of the situation.

The I Ching should prevent you from falling into the way of truisms, because the answer you get is unique to this moment. It becomes a question of what you bring to the moment: are you able to delve beneath the obvious characteristics of the situation to deeper layers, to something important to you? Are you able to see a different point of view that is helpful to you? Can you be comforted or warned by its words?

When we go forward, from moment to moment, we may find it helpful to be optimistic. "Today I expect good things to come my way." "The people I meet will be charming and fun to be with." Optimism would seem to be a better outlook than pessimism.

I consider the hexagram 44: Kou: Coming to Meet. The commentator I read, R.L. Wing, said, "A seemingly harmless but potentially dangerous temptation has entered the picture. It appears trifling, but it could seize control and cause chaos." I find this forthright, even bold, as bold as the suggestion it is presenting. I would need to take stock of what it might mean for me.

It could refer to a specific person: a strong, assertive woman (or man) who could charm us and use us to pursue their own ends. It could refer to a class of people and a way of life that goes with it: going out dancing every night, or constantly going to entertainments, or being immersed in a life of indulgence. Conversely, it could refer to letting slip patterns of self-discipline, self-care and self-awareness.

I compare what R.L. Wing says with the most concise rendering of the hexagrams that I have, the I Ching Cards by Agmuller, 1971 (based on the James Legge translation). For 44, it simply says, "Kou shows a female who is bold and strong. It will not be good to marry such a female."

Wilhelm refers to the trigrams: Heaven is above Wind, which means that there is a single broken line at the bottom and there are five firm lines above it. "Of its own accord the female principle comes to meet the male. It is an unfavourable and dangerous situation, and we must understand and promptly prevent the possible consequences."

The judgement says: "Coming to meet. The maiden is powerful. One should not marry such a maiden." What Wing says echoes what is said in Wilhelm's commentary. Note that Wilhelm refers to the "female principle", so he is extending the meaning beyond the particular image of a strong woman making an approach to a man and the man being beguiled. We are to consider other situations to which the concept may apply. It may also stand for an unworthy person approaching the king, or seeking to cultivate favour at the court.

Alfred Huang analyses the ideograph and what it adds to the name and judgement of the hexagram. He applies this to a story about King Wen and his quest to overcome the tyrannical Shang emperor. Huang also has a section on each hexagram that discusses its significance. Here he observes that the ancient sages adopted a conciliatory attitude towards unexpected people who approached, but considered whether they should take preventive measures.

Huang refers again to King Wen to note that in his situation, evil forces had been eliminated but their influence had not entirely faded. Thus, what was happening now was a continuation of that effort. He also notes that King Wen did not show animosity to the persons encountered, but likewise showed no tolerance.

Stephen Karcher brings a different slant to this hexagram. It represents the return of feminine power, the occurrence of strange encounters; it stands for copulation. It says to welcome what comes, but do not try to grasp it and hang onto it. This brief encounter connects you to a creative force. The wind below heaven spreads throughout the world.

Yet another perspective is offered by Hua-Ching Ni. He begins with the trigrams: Heaven is above the Wind: the wind touches everything in its course, and the situation appears smooth. But danger is indicated by the negative line at the bottom approaching the five strong lines. So, he says, "One should be careful of this situation and heed the warning of this hexagram."

He sees it as five men competing for the one woman, and observes that one strong woman can break up the unity of the five men. He also discusses this from the perspective of the woman: she must act well if the outcome is to be peaceful.

However, he looks beyond this scenario. The hexagram also stands for any situation where darkness re-enters, and there is propensity for the strong to misjudge it and allow it to advance. This can apply in a social group, and it also applies to one's inner space. In social situations, there is a need for the strong parties to cooperate with each other. In personal situations, he says, problems grow larger through neglect.

Hua-Ching Ni also offers a section of commentary on the significance of the hexagram, which sometimes consists of a lengthy story about his personal life. His father was a doctor in China, and a man of some wisdom and influence. He taught his son what he could, from the old philosophies and from his experiences in life. Hua-Ching Ni was an eager pupil, and he endeavoured to show his father how much he had learned.

One time, his father said to him, "What you say is not the practice of the true mind. The practice of the true mind is not the practice of criticism. In all the examples you mentioned, there is the opportunity for the important practice of non-bewilderment within any confused situation. In other words, the practice of true mind on these occasions is clarity. The true mind is responsive, but it does not lose its clarity."

With this advice, Hua-Ching Ni continued on his way. He came back to his father later and gave him another account of his experiences. This time his father said, "Be careful, son. Clarity is only one virtue of the true mind. There are other equally important practices of the true mind, such as sincerity, freedom from temptation, non-evasion, composure and peace, non-dissipation, dispassion, unattachment, and harmony, among many other virtues."

In reading this passage, I realised that Hua-Ching Ni's father was not giving his son a comprehensive list of the virtues of a true mind (which I note, I have not tried to define). It was a list of the virtues he thought of at that moment. On another occasion the list of virtues would be different. This was something new to accept: one's self-development is not dependent on having a perfect, comprehensive list of the virtues (which would be static). From moment to moment we just have the expression of it that is relevant to the moment, or best for the moment. This is the nature of it.

This is to realise how pervasive our "western" minds are. I have a book in my library about character and the virtues, and it offers twenty-four virtues. I have a leadership book that discusses leadership development in terms of sixty-nine characteristics – competencies and virtues. I have myself, in the ethics books I have written, tried to produce a list of virtues, driven by the idea that there is (probably) a comprehensive list that contains all of them.

There may be relevance in my lists of virtues, as a way of indicating the extent and shape of the field, but that is the essential point: I have to see the lists as indicative only, not definitive. What difference does this make? What I notice in Hua-Ching Ni's father's statement is his confidence. He understands the true mind so well that the next time he needs to offer a list of its relevant virtues, he will have it readily to hand, and it may very well be different to the previous list he offered, yet it will be just as pertinent and illuminating.

Do I recommend any particular translations or commentaries? In some cases you can see that little thought has been put into a publication, and in other cases you may not like a book, no matter how much thought has been put into it. You can put those books aside. But on the other hand, you may need to spend a lot of time with a book to develop an appropriate appreciation for it.

One could say, this is how one develops true mind.

33 A viewpoint from Taiwan

I have another book in my collection, called *The I Ching and You*. The author is Diana ffarington Hook. Her books were published in England in the 1970s, but her acknowledgments are to I Ching scholars in Taiwan. This book is not a translation of the I Ching nor a commentary on it. Rather, it is a workbook on how to use it. She suggests using Richard Wilhelm's version for consultation.

The copy I have of Hook's book includes a little cardboard pocket that has been stuck to the inside front cover, which contains three coins for consulting the I Ching. This was obviously added by the book's previous owner. They are lovely old Chinese coins with the square hole in the middle. The book also has an "ex libris" (from the library of...) sticker on the page, with the owner's name. It was originally purchased from the Adyar Bookshop in Sydney.

Hook says the I Ching is a book of life containing an explanation of the entire laws of the universe, and directions on how man should conduct himself so as to remain in harmony with these laws. If we become out of harmony with it, the result is sickness and misery. Hook quotes Jung (from Wilhelm's book): "The meanings of the hexagrams are engraved in the collective unconscious of the human race, and when you toss the coins you are simply activating the age-old wisdom of the universal subconscious which dwells in all men."

Hook filters the I Ching through a strongly Christian perspective, but she says that through regular, practical use of the I Ching, one may transform one's entire existence. The book may be used for practical guidance on everyday problems in life, as a lead for furthering one's knowledge of oneself, and as a basis for meditation.

The book explores several themes in the I Ching. One throws the coins and obtains one or two hexagrams, but one also has to see the hexagram within the sequence of all the hexagrams. If one obtains 44, as above, one must know how it fits into the sequence, for this is a part of an overall narrative. In Hook's version of the narrative, we can start at 40, which is a time of Deliverance, which is followed by Decrease (41), but this is followed by Increase (42). Directly before 44 is 43, which is Breakthrough, while 44 is Coming to Meet. 44 is followed by 45, Gathering Together.

Other writers often use different names for the hexagrams. The implication is that they tell the whole story in a slightly different way, much as observers will describe a picture differently.

It should be noted that there are two forms of the sequencing of the hexagrams. The one just described is the numerical sequence, which is how the hexagrams are numbered and how they are presented in the book (both Wilhelm's and others). However, the second way of showing the hexagrams is the circular sequence. This refers to the thought forms behind the hexagrams. These are based on Fu Hsi's original trigrams, and how the trigrams evolve from one to another. This is usually shown in a diagram.

Both sequences show that together, the hexagrams form a coordinated whole. One can track through the hexagrams in the numerical sequence and follow the changes in the lines of the trigrams and see that this follows a pattern.

Hook provides several diagrams showing the hexagrams in an overall pattern. She also discusses the meaning of the lines in the hexagrams, and their relationship to each other. This is more detailed than looking simply at the trigrams. I have found it best to follow the commentators and the level of detail they choose to offer. This means that any abstract knowledge I accumulate is given in the context of a particular hexagram.

It is a question of whether one wants to be an authority on the I Ching as a complex system, or whether one wants to keep the focus on the content. I prefer the latter. I am following the story.

34 Beginning: 3: Zhun

Sometimes, the I Ching has given me the hexagram 3: Beginning: Zhun, and I wonder, "Am I at the beginning of something?" And the image of Beginning is turbulent: Water is above Thunder. The beginning is not peaceful, controlled and leisurely, as if you were starting out on a short hike on a sunny day. No; there is rain falling from above, and there is thunder booming. One has to struggle to move forward through this turbulence.

The image is of sprouting, of life coming into being. It takes great energy for it to make its way into the open. But also, one must remember that before the sprout breaks through the surface of the soil, its roots have been growing downwards. Life suddenly appears, but it has already been growing. So too with us.

Another aspect is that the sprout is tender, but it has had the strength to break through the soil. It has penetrated obstacles. We should trust in our own strength, and not think that we are weak and helpless.

The interaction of thunder and the water makes us think of confusion, so it is good to remember that the movement is from chaos to order. All living things follow this path towards the fulfilment of their innate nature.

The sprout also reminds us that despite its tough passage into the light, it has still met with conditions congenial to growth. This growth will continue, but it is better if we remain conscious of the growth, and not be complacent about it. And it is better that we remain connected with our root. This is our bond with heaven and earth.

The various translators express this differently, but the train of thought is similar. Deng Ming-Dao says that at the time of Beginning, the noble one considers his/her principles.

I, having considered all that ensues from Beginning, turn back to my circumstances. I am at the beginning of dealing with the news that I had a slight stroke. In one sense it is ridiculous; I am feeling okay, and I have no obvious impairments. On the other hand, there is an MRI scan that says I have spots of bleeding in my brain. There is an implied threat that something worse could/will happen to me.

There is thunder booming and rain falling.

I am working my way through the "brain book" (*The Brain's Way of Healing*) and the stories are galling. The people described have had terrible things happen to them. Their detriments have been significant, their recoveries have been truly hard, and their determination has been awesome. But they have indeed recovered, some from injuries, some from disease.

The pathways of their recoveries have been different. Some have employed technological devices. Some have undertaken exercises for the brain. I am interested in meditation and visualisation. I am interested in awareness. I am interested in controlling what is happening to me. Managing it, mastering it. I do not wish to fall into a dependent medical regime for the rest of my life.

I am aware that today our society is dominated by medicine as an industry rather than as a profession. And to be brutally honest, an industry is not interested in people being cured; it is interested in ongoing business – dependency. At the top of these pyramids of medical options – repeat appointments, more tests, data collection, surgery, medicines, dosages – are some very rich people. There is also the largely undiscussed collateral damage of side effects.

However, I also have to be careful about not becoming a "grumpy old man" or bitter. Another hexagram I drew recently was 15: Modesty. Here, the Mountain is below the Earth. The mountain usually towers above the earth, but here it has placed itself below earth, in an act of humility. This is a most important virtue in the I Ching. Deng Ming-Dao says: "Mountain, Earth: none makes a show, and yet each lives powerfully and long."

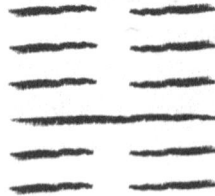

35 Reasons to keep using the I Ching

Diana ffarington Hook suggests that once you have used the I Ching for a while, the images are internalised. The effect of this is that you may not need to throw the coins so often, because when you find yourself in a situation, you already have an idea of what themes are relevant to it.

This is true. Nevertheless, there may still be value in throwing the coins. For a start, as I have frequently found, the answer may surprise you. And they may certainly add to the ideas that have been floating around your mind. My desire is to learn the I Ching more deeply. There is a value in it beyond the particular situation in which I find myself.

When I threw the coins (recently) and obtained the hexagram 44: Coming to Meet, I also obtained a second hexagram, 6: Conflict. When someone seemingly harmless has approached you, and you are tempted to enter into a dalliance – and this may be true at a metaphorical level as well, you may follow the situation into conflict. The movement from hexagram 44 to hexagram 6 came because of a single moving line.

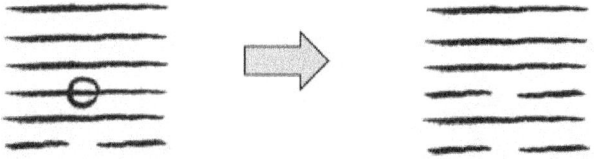

44: Coming to Meet: Gou   6: Conflict: Song

The moving line said, "You are tempted, but you are held back in spite of yourself. However, you are in a state of indecision and you need to resolve it." Accordingly, I read what was said in hexagram 6. It raised questions for me.

The essence of hexagram 6 is that in a conflict situation, you should not think that the way forward is through aggression. Pushing brashly forward does not tend to lead to lasting success. We may dream of a crushing victory, but the message here is that that approach will cause obstinacy, not the cooperative will to resolve the problem.

That is part of the message. The other part is that you need to examine your own mindset. You may believe that your proposed path is correct and every other path is wrong, and you want to proceed confidently. But if you do so, the conflict is certain. Instead, this is the time to look at your situation from another perspective. For example, in a conflict with another person, you need to ponder whether that person also thinks they are correct.

In this circumstance, appealing to an external authority may enable a resolution to be obtained that will bring peace to all. In the legal system, this means to use a magistrate or judge. More broadly, a counsellor may help.

I am thinking of my odd situation with the medical issue. Already the doctors have a variety of opinions, and I am reading a relevant book as well. The point would be to consider what would a sound understanding of what is happening be? Can one of the doctors or specialists persuade me that they know something helpful? Will I read something in the book that I can apply, and learn from experience?

One lesson for me would be to try not to alienate any of the doctors in this indeterminate time. In the commentary I chose (it was R.L. Wing), I read, "Avoid unresolvable disagreements; be ready to compromise. Do not try to force the issue. And personally reconsider your beliefs and practices."

In reading through this judgement, I can see why one keeps consulting the I Ching. There is much to learn. The effort is day by day, and the issues keep changing shape. Especially if one is taking action, grandly or modestly, and trying to stay on track, the I Ching continues to offer its guidance.

The day after I obtained Conflict (6), I got the hexagram 16: Enthusiasm. In this hexagram, things are moving ahead smoothly. All things in nature follow the path of least resistance. One illustration of this is that the sun, the moon and the earth all follow their orbits in the sky. And in societies, there are customs and traditions as people follow their familiar patterns.

Another example is music. The melodies and harmonies are patterns of sound that attract people by inspiring them. Through music, people harmonise their spirits with the cosmic order. It instils in their bodies an enthusiasm for life.

I love music, so it was easy for me to take this message in. What was unexpected, however, was that the next chapter I read in the brain book was about music. The story was about how a teacher/therapist used music to foster healing in the brain of a young man.

I often find numerous such occurrences in my daily life. It is as if life is dancing, or waving a wand – touching this, then touching that, weaving a long thread through time.

36 Synchronicity

I have mentioned synchronicity, but it is necessary to talk about it further. Jung mentions it in his Foreword to Wilhelm's I Ching. It is a central principle in the I Ching. Whereas the West is concerned with determining causality between objects and events, the philosophy behind the I Ching is focused on the idea that there is a peculiar interdependence between things, something more than chance. It likewise exists in the subjective states of people. Jung says it is as if the Chinese mind focused on the very things that the Western mind ignores.

It was Jung who gave this phenomenon the term "synchronicity". It could be defined as the occurrence of meaningful coincidences that seem to have no cause. We use the term to refer to times when events seem to conspire to tell us something, and even teach us something. There seems to be a confluence between an external event and our inner state. It is as if our lives constitute a novel, and this is a significant twist in the plot.

It may be that our life at that time is not the one that we dream it is. For example, we may be telling ourselves that we have a great job, but in fact, at a deep level, we are not happy, or we don't think this is the life we were meant to live. Accordingly, we may resist the coincidence; we may deny or dismiss it. The very randomness of the event may offend us. In this way, the emotional impact of a synchronous event is often significant.

Jung saw that the phenomenon would come to be of more interest as modern physics developed, as it was aware of life as a flow of energy rather than a collection of material objects. Also, it examined life at a much finer level, observing phenomena that we had previously had no idea about.

For him it was not that we had proven there were no connections, or causal connections, between certain things, but that we had no way of demonstrating the causality. In fact, the coincidences only make sense if we see them as acausal. So, he asserted that for the Chinese mind, the question of finding causality had no interest. The thing to do was to consider the meaning of the connections.

There is a literature on synchronicity, some of it from the perspective of psychology, and some of it arguing for the link between synchronicity and modern physics. Jung wrote *Synchronicity: An Acausal Connecting Principle*, published in 1952, helping Western culture to accept the phenomenon, even if it could not be understood with a scientific approach.

Robert Hopcke, a psychotherapist, wrote about synchronicity under the title, *There Are No Accidents* (1997). He presents many stories of synchronicity: stories of love, stories in the workplace, and stories about dreams. He asks the question, how do we use these events constructively, as turning points that lead us toward a more meaningful life? The very idea that an event might be synchronistic gives you a different perspective. It is as if you are suddenly looking at your life from a higher level.

Hopcke mentions the I Ching, recognising that people use the randomness of its method to tap into an expanded meaning of their life. He also notes that there is a variety of tools and methods, such as the Tarot, and they may be variously considered philosophical, spiritual, magical, folk lore, or superstitious.

However, the difficulty of accepting synchronicity remains for many people. It is because, in our culture, we are dominated by the idea that the world is constructed out of the operation of cause and effect. We are accustomed to thinking that everything that happens is a result of causes, and it has set in motion a continuing chain of causes and effects. It means that we have a part to play in this world in that chain of causes and effects.

Synchronicity does not annihilate this world or deny it, but it expands the world to include things that we cannot explain, and it indicates that there may be many connections between things that we cannot see and are not aware of. It shifts us from the position that we control our world (and I need to contemplate this too). And yet it invites us to think there is meaning at work here: everything is not meaningless.

We try to eliminate chance, but the idea of synchronicity invites us to recognise the possibility of it and allow it to be, accepting that it may offer opportunities and breakthroughs. The greater truth is that we are not isolated individuals, but rather, we live as part of a web in which everyone and everything participates.

If this is so, then the way to live in this environment is to be aware, to discern when it is the right time to act, to constantly examine your own attitude, and to accept the support of the wider community. Overall, one must develop a sense of the whole, of all-that-is. One may call it the divine, and then one sees the need for humility. The emphasis in this environment has shifted away from individual domination towards service.

This is the kind of picture Hopcke paints. It is very much like the kind of picture that develops when you use the I Ching regularly. Hopcke says that paying attention to coincidences in our lives, and being alert to synchronicity, reminds us that our lives are a story. This is to say that our lives have a coherence and a direction, and we have a reason for being. We are part of something larger than ourselves, and it is a thing of great beauty.

Another offering on synchronicity is from Joseph Jaworski (which Hopcke includes in his bibliography). He is the founder of the American Leadership Forum. He relates the concepts of synchronicity to leadership. His book is called *Synchronicity: The Inner Path of Leadership* (2011).

Jaworski is interested in the qualities of leaders and the elements of leadership development. He does not come to the topic of synchronicity from the perspective of the I Ching. But what does he say?

He believes we have the capacity to sense what is emerging in our situations (what Geoffrey Redmond called incipience), and to shape the future instead of just reacting to what happens to us. He says that we can access the wisdom we need for constructive action. In taking this approach, he has questioned the dominant scientific-materialistic viewpoint of our society. He does not reject that point of view, but he says it is no longer adequate, and a more comprehensive worldview is emerging.

Jaworski thinks there is an underlying intelligence within the universe, and it is "capable of guiding us and preparing us for the futures we must create". He thinks there are hidden potentials lying dormant in the universe, and we carry the power to change the world as we know it. To do this, we need to shift the prevailing belief system.

His book starts with Carl Jung's description of synchronicity. In Jaworski's case he is talking about peak moments when it seems as if we are being helped by hidden hands. Jaworski was intrigued by this phenomenon and decided to study it. He came to the view that we have the capacity to see and to participate in "an unfolding creative order". Likewise, we can lose this flow or destroy it, so it is important to work with it consciously.

The structure of the book is based on Joseph Campbell's concept of the hero's journey: life as a heroic quest. Jaworski sets out the four stages: 1) preparing to journey, 2) crossing the threshold, 3) the hero's journey, and 4) the gift. In the beginning there is a call to adventure, but one does this from within an inauthentic life. The second stage begins when we say "yes" to the call. We find that we often obtain help on the road. The third stage is an ordeal that tests our commitment but also presses us to learn from our failures. The fourth stage is the fulfilment of the quest and the gift of accomplishment.

Peter Senge, who wrote the introduction to Jaworski's book, said that the most important book on leadership was Robert Greenleaf's book on "Servant Leadership", which argued that the leader's job was to serve the whole (the group, the organisation, the community, the society). But Jaworski has extended this notion further, saying that to acknowledge synchronicity is to choose to serve life. And this is "to allow life to unfold through me".

Through living in awareness of synchronicity, one comes to a deepening understanding of how the universe works, and acquires an increased capacity for participating in the unfolding of the world. And the learning of this is not an intellectual exercise; one must learn it through one's experience of life. One must live it in order to learn. But a story may help one to map out the terrain. Accordingly, Jaworski offers a story grounded in his own life.

Apparently, Greenleaf, the author of *Servant Leadership* (1977), drew on Herman Hesse's story, *Journey to the East*. Senge comments that most books on leadership offer theories, principles and advice. In contrast, Greenleaf, and Jaworski, tell us the story of their journey to understanding. The message is that our own learning will be the story of our lives.

This change in understanding occurs in the midst of an overriding social environment of helplessness combined with ceaseless activity. But, through a shift in our perspective, we can take a different view of the present. Through the things that happen, and our openness to our experiences, we can accept the possibilities of life. It means that we forego the feelings of helplessness and the urge to work ceaselessly (out of desperation) to achieve goals. It means that we understand that life is constantly emerging. When the leaves on the tree rustle, we know there is a wind. The effects of the unseen wind manifest.

The books on synchronicity bring to mind Richard Rudd's threefold view of the hexagrams in the I Ching. Humans are born into Shadow, such as the environment today: a feeling of helplessness combined with a felt need for ceaseless activity to achieve goals which we hope will banish the feeling of helplessness. But there is a Gift level, where we feel that life contains possibility, and that we have the power to work creatively with what surrounds us. And there is the Siddhi level, which is an expression of bliss and oneness.

From the perspective that Rudd offers, we can say that synchronicity is a quality of the gift level. (The Siddhi level is a more intense expression of emerging consciousness.)

The I Ching is a pathway. There are other pathways too. As has been said: "There are many pathways up the mountain; the view from the top is the same."

37 Philosophy, or not?

Does the I Ching convey a philosophy? You could say that this question only leads us into a semantic argument. *The Shorter Oxford English Dictionary* has, as you might expect, a pretty array of definitions of philosophy. Most broadly, it is the love of wisdom or knowledge, both theoretical and practical. Alternatively, it is the knowledge or study of the principles of human action or conduct. Or, it is the department of knowledge or study which deals with ultimate reality, or with the most general causes and principles of things.

Or, it refers to a philosophical system or theory. Or, it refers to the system a person forms for the conduct of their life. Does the I Ching present such a philosophy of life? On the face of it, it would not seem so. It is a compendium of sixty-four hexagrams, the commentary on them, and the imagery associated with them.

Joseph Jaworski said that the concept of synchronicity made a difference to the way he lived his life, and his book was an account of how that change occurred, told through a life story. And, he said, it was not until he was preparing the second edition of the book that he started to think about what the underlying principles were, and could begin to articulate them.

In a similar way, does the I Ching *contain* a philosophy? One could use alternative language. In the field of ethics, Timothy Chappell (*Ethics and Experience*, 2009) talks about developing an "ethical outlook". He describes this as having a coherent and consistent "set of views and commitments about the central questions concerning value: what is worth living for and what is worth dying for; what is really admirable and what is really contemptible; what must we do at all costs and what must we not do no matter what."

I think Chappell's recommendation is admirable. We might ask, then, does the I Ching give this to us? Certainly the I Ching speaks out of an ethical perspective. It continually admonishes us to be "steadfast and upright". But it also infers things about the nature of the world. In hexagram 1 it says, "The movement of heaven is full of power." In hexagram 2 it says, "The earth's condition is receptive devotion."

However, in saying this, we have to recognise that these statements refer to the images of the hexagrams; these are not intended to be hard-edged scientific statements, that is, literal statements about the material nature of the world.

We could talk about developing an outlook on life informed by the I Ching. But I don't think this makes much difference. The word "outlook" is simply a proxy for having a philosophy.

But first, we should note the language that Jaworski uses. He talks about experiencing synchronicity as a capacity that he developed, as opposed to the scientific-materialistic worldview. He refers to it as a transformation, and as something deeper than a cognitive outlook. It involves moral values, and a subtle level of personal development.

One writer who discusses the philosophical aspect of the I Ching is Carol Anthony, in *The Philosophy of the I Ching* (1981). She takes the view that the I Ching is not a philosophy: "It is no system of belief, nor is it a systematised explanation of our existence." The explanation it contains "avoids making a philosophical statement." Rather, she says, the I Ching helps us to solve problems, and it "guides us to an understanding of the higher life of the spirit".

She goes on to say "our understanding does not come by way of intellectual study, but through experiences that cause us to penetrate the deepest reaches of our intuitive awareness. In time, we learn to depend on that awareness as the most appropriate basis for action." This seems similar to what Jaworski says about his experience with synchronicity. It is also similar to what I would say. Over time, the practice of using the I Ching opens up a new way of seeing the world; it *becomes* the way you see the world.

One of the things that Anthony says is that we should not approach the I Ching as if we were an objective critic, standing outside it and formulating an opinion. The only way to learn what it has to teach is to immerse ourselves in it. As Richard Rudd expressed it: "You need to be a lover of mystery with a beginner's mind, rather than arriving as an expert determined to solve a puzzle."

Much of the discussion about whether or not the I Ching is a philosophy starts from the idea of philosophy as an intellectual occupation. The Oxford dictionary itself comes out of this tradition. The distinction made is between the intellect and the feelings. Once the framework has been constructed in this way, the options are limited. It may be more helpful to use the framework used by Peter Senge in his book, *The Fifth Discipline* (1990).

Senge discusses the idea of expertise, and the idea that an expert possesses certain qualities. They are part of his/her nature, not simply "stuck on"; nor is the situation adequately described by saying the expert possesses certain knowledge. Much of what the expert knows may be tacit, that is, embodied but not explicit or able to be put into words.

The path to expertise generally begins with following rules and procedures, long before the person has any understanding of why they are used. The next stage is when the person begins to understand the principles behind the rules, and is able to generalise and adapt actions across other contexts. Next, the person begins to integrate the principles into their person, and acquire values that apply to the field of endeavour. The person has not simply acquired some compartmentalised skills and habits; they have changed as a person.

This model may make more sense of what happens over time as a person uses the I Ching, rather than letting the emphasis fall on the concept of philosophy. And as the word "integration" implies, there is no longer any hard distinction between knowledge and values. The person acquires an outlook that is part and parcel of how the person sees the world. It is rather different to merely having an opinion about something. The way the person acts is integrated with the way the world makes sense.

However, the need to have a philosophy that can be expressed can be admitted. Hua-Ching Ni talks about the troubles of the world today, and how a healthier approach is needed (as noted earlier). We have been very successful in developing new technologies, but we are faced with the threat of potential destruction. We have mastered all spheres of life, but we are overwhelmed by our creations.

We lack a correct way of thinking, we lack inner development, and it is too easy for people who are merely ambitious to seize positions of power. We need to return to the question of what nurtures our minds and hearts, and guides our spirit. We have not yet arrived at insights sufficient to ensure a secure future.

Hua-Ching Ni maintains that the I Ching serves this purpose. As an ancient store of wisdom, it "teaches us how to look for the most appropriate point in any particular behaviour or event." It offers "clarity in the mental sphere, balance in daily life, and positive, steady spiritual growth". He goes on to say, "A bright new epoch starts with a correct philosophy that can guide people to restore human nature to its original healthy condition and then encourage them to attain further development."

It was said of Confucius that he never spelled out the whole message of a teaching; that he might say twenty percent of the message and leave it to you to find the other eighty percent. This way you would retain what you learned, and it would be your own learning. Following this logic, we might say that the I Ching may not spell out a philosophy, but it is there for you to find.

Moreover, among people who study the I Ching, the message is the same. Again, it is like studying a painting. People may gain different insights, but those insights are shared, and a similar understanding forms among them.

38 Emergent philosophy

Two views are in tension. One says that the I Ching is the same as it ever was. If you go back to the essence – the trigrams – you could say it has been the same for five thousand years: Heaven, Earth, Water, Fire, and so on. The other view is that it has been evolving since then, in stages. King Wen and the Duke of Zhou paired the trigrams to make sixty-four hexagrams around three thousand years ago; and Confucius added the Ten Wings commentary in around 500 BC.

After that we have over two thousand years of usage where commentary was added, and commentary was perhaps modified. Scholars added their perspectives. John Minford, for example, bases his book on Wilhelm's translation, but he adds commentary from scholars from over the last two thousand years. It is erudite, delightful, and illuminating.

We have seen that there are arguments about what was the "original" version of the I Chïng, before people started "adding to it". For example, some people argue that Confucius's commentary is not part of the I Ching, and they reject it vehemently, thinking they have found a "purer" version of it. I, on the other hand, accept the flowering of the I Ching over history.

There can be arguments about language and particular words, but there can also be arguments about the overall philosophy. Considering all the people who have produced books on the I Ching in our own lifetime, are they speaking from some common core?

There is no doubt that the people who have written books on the I Ching come from a wide variety of perspectives. The pertinent question to ask oneself is, after a period using a particular book, are you finding that it is helpful? Of course it may challenge you at times; this is in the nature of the I Ching, but is the book a helpful companion?

We must remember that the people who have written a book on the I Ching are human and therefore are still learning themselves. Beyond this, there is a question of whether insights into the I Ching are still emerging, and the overall philosophy could be called (after five thousand years) emergent.

In an essential way, the trigrams are the same as they ever were: mountain is still mountain, lake is still lake. It is a question of what we see in them. The meanings are ours to meditate on, and we inevitably relate them to our own life experience and our contemporary culture. This is ground that is as fertile as it ever was. Moreover, this is only the beginning; the heart of the I Ching is in the relationships between the trigrams. For an individual, the I Ching is an ever-deepening lake, an ever-ascending mountain.

It is another thing to ponder what the overall view of the I Ching is. We may observe that it is evolving because people have come to it from modern perspectives. Richard Rudd has married the I Ching to the findings of biology and DNA. Jung brought the perspective of depth psychology to the I Ching. Some writers apply what the I Ching says to organisational contexts.

The sub-title of Hua-Ching Ni's book is "The book of changes and the unchanging truth". He says the goal of all teaching is the Subtle Essence. It is the deep truth of all religions, yet it leaves religion behind. It does not belong to the emotional surface of life, and it is not confined by thought or belief.

Ni offers the I Ching as the means of learning the Subtle Essence. It expresses the pure minds of the ancients that can provide us with the insight we need today. It can guide us through the trials of life. It is not a dogma or a doctrine. Instead, it invites us to look for the appropriate point in any situation. Then one learns what is appropriate and can incorporate it into one's thought processes.

The I Ching is a philosophy insofar as it guides people to restore them to their original nature, healthy and alive. It then enables them to attain further development. Ni says the I Ching was one of ancient man's first successes in finding the laws which regulate all phenomena, and discovering that since nature and humanity are one, harmony is the key to life. A balanced way of life is the fundamental path. In contrast, modern humanity obscures the significance of nature.

Ni concludes that our study of the I Ching, its hexagrams and lines, is the way to understand the underlying nature of people and events.

This call to the wisdom of the ancients contrasts with the idea that today we are seeing a new conversation about the nature of the world. Until modern science gave us a vastly different history of the universe, we accepted that the earth was just a backdrop to human affairs, and we assumed that it was unchanging. Christianity offered a picture of the past informed by the Bible, understood literally, beginning in the Garden of Eden. But philosophers also held a fixed picture of the world. Immanuel Kant (1714-1804), for example, took the world to be an unchanging backdrop to the human quest for meaning, truth and goodness.

Our view of the natural world has extended to nearly fourteen billion years, and includes the long history of life on our planet and its evolution. John Haught (*The New Cosmic Story*, 2017) argues that this picture of the physical universe has now become the whole story, and the story of humans as a locus of subjectivity has been swept aside. Haught is a champion of religion because it asserts "the existence of an interior life [consciousness] and of the need to undergo awakening and transformation."

The point of Haught's stance is that the story of the universe is a story that is as yet unfinished. As such, it is an emergent one. He says it makes a difference to look at the universe this way. This perspective means that he looks at the history of religions as significant events in human history. He refers specifically to the time between 800 and 300 BC when numerous new religions came into being across the world: China, India, Europe and the Near East.

He mentions the *Tao Te Ching* from China. What he says generally is that around this time, religions shifted their concerns from rituals, petitions and appeasement of supernatural beings to personal awakening and spiritual transformation. "The purpose of our lives, they taught, is to awaken to this hidden realm of being and allow our lives to be transformed by it…. The new wave of consciousness began to make sharper distinctions than ever before between a right way and a wrong way to live, think, act, work, and pray."

Hua-Ching Ni would support the idea that the I Ching was part of this revolution. He would say that our subjectivity is implicit in the physical universe. Haught says that modern science has shown the reality of this subjectivity, although many intellectuals with an historical or scientific bias hold to the position that the world is meaningless.

Haught sets out his position as follows: "Without a profound sense that there exists, already and forever, an indestructible rightness towards which the universe is turning, our sense of meaning, truth, goodness and beauty would be groundless. Without a sense, however, that our own lives along with the whole cosmic process can contribute something new and indispensable to the 'realising' of rightness, these same lives – and the whole cosmic story – would lack significance" (p. 28).

I suggest that this philosophy is implicit in the I Ching, and this shines through in the most commendable translations of the book.

39 The need for morality

The I Ching is about the nature of the world, but it is also about morality. It urges us to be steadfast and upright. It presents an image of the admirable person (the superior person, the noble one, the true gentleman, the sage). The crux of moral arguments is that we are seldom in the position of being able to enforce moral rules in society. The I Ching recognises this and offers counsel for living uprightly and also not suffering unduly from the actions of unethical people.

It is straightforward enough for us to make rules for society or for groups of people. Hence we have constitutions, laws and policies. Likewise we can set punishments for wrongdoing. One can assume that if the lawmakers are people of goodwill, are well-informed, and are of moderate intelligence, things will go well.

However, much more needs to be said. From the ruler's (or government's, or leader's) point of view, can we encourage right-doing? Can we inspire people, or nudge them, or teach them, why and how to be good?

From the viewpoint of an ordinary person, not having any particular power or authority, how does one survive in an imperfect world? It seems that one relies on the goodwill of those around us, and on luck.

The I Ching recognises that we can face many different kinds of situations. Some of them will be favourable; some of them will be daunting. We need to be ready for all of this. Often, our attitude will make a difference to how the situation develops. Here are some examples.

The hexagram that seems quite relevant is 10: Conduct: Lu. I have mentioned this before (Chapter 3), but there are aspects worth commenting on here. The central image is of a person who, in innocence, treads on the tail of a tiger, but it does not bite him/her. What does it mean?

It seems to say that the world can be a dangerous place; the tiger is a dangerous creature that can kill us. One would think that the situation is clear-cut: if you come across a tiger, it will bite you and kill you. But that doesn't happen here. Somehow, the tiger does not do what you would expect it to do. The tiger would not even be acting evilly; it would simply be doing what tigers do. It reflects the nature of the world. (The I Ching is very clear-eyed about the nature of the world.)

Why does the tiger not bite? There are clues in the commentary (I am reading from Wilhelm and Hua-Ching Ni). Although one has trodden on the tail of the tiger, one has still been exercising caution. One has not been acting in a bombastic way that leads to trouble. The six lines form Heaven above and Lake below. The lake is soft and gentle, and it can easily be overcome by the power of heaven, thus it realises that it is best to seek harmony in relationships.

Further, the person trusts her own nature, and does not force herself on others, seeking glory, or demanding favours. She has strength within. Richard Rudd's presentation of the tenth gene key names the gift as Naturalness. It is about how to "be yourself" after you have overcome the shadow of self-obsession. Initially, this may be accompanied by some vestiges of fear. It is as if, when I try to be natural, I may step on the tail of a tiger.

This discussion brings us to the conclusion that proper conduct is connected with the idea of acting naturally, but it is a naturalness that is free of ego. Morality, then, is not compliance with a set of rules (which would, of course, be strict and severe), but living as we were meant to live. And so, Wilhelm says, "The superior person fortifies the thinking of the people."

When I threw the coins and got the hexagram 10, there was a moving line, and the hexagram changed to 61: Inner Truth: Zhong Fu. It seemed fitting that we should go from Conduct to Inner Truth. Hexagram 61 has two broken lines in the middle, and four firm lines outside. One of the images for the hexagram is an egg, with the shell outside and the life within.

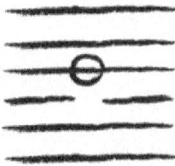

10: Conduct: Lu   61: Inner Truth: Zhong Fu

The trigrams are Wind above Lake. We are reminded that the wind is invisible, but its effects are seen. It is like spirit, and so much of life: there has to have been something there, or there would have been no effect. The lake is joyous and the wind above is gentle: Inner Truth. What does it mean? The two broken lines give us emptiness in the middle. Taoism says that everything comes from emptiness: "The Tao is an empty vessel: it is used but never filled." (Ch. 4)

From Inner Truth, one can achieve great things. It furthers one to cross the great stream. From Inner Truth, one can establish bonds with other people, but these bonds must be more than having common interests. Thieves have comrades, but only because they have common interests. If they ceased to be a thief, their friends would no longer be their friends. The person of inner truth will create true bonds that are based on what is right, what is steadfast.

The person of inner truth is not weak, but they have great clarity. In these comments, we see that life is about more than morality, but morality is the foundation of life. In his other comments, Wilhelm says there may be obstacles. There are challenges in life, and there is work to do. All is not perfect. To overcome obstacles, we must learn how to work with other people, how to understand them, how to influence and teach them, and how to do this with compassion.

40 Further thoughts on morality and thriving

Consulting the I Ching regularly becomes a narrative. It opens up new directions in my thinking and feeling. After I received Conduct (10) and Inner Truth (61), the coins gave me Seeking Harmony (13) followed by Abundance (55). The message one receives is personal, not a generic truth. For me, 13 contains both an offering and a caution.

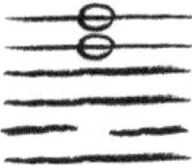

13: Seeking Harmony: Tong Ren

55: Abundance: Feng

I am attracted to the image of the hermit: living alone and working out my own issues by myself, and also, not being dependent on social contact with other people. I think there is merit in this, and to a point it is appropriate. However, the I Ching suggests that it is not inappropriate to have connections with other humans.

As well as being called "Seeking Harmony", 13 is called "Fellowship". I read what John Minford had to say. The inference of his commentary was, it is all very well to talk about personal development, but when one extends one's thought to the state of the world, one has to recognise that the world as a whole has an aspiration. Minford says the world wishes to be one community, and the true gentleman can imagine this one community as a place of love and sincerity, a place where the talents of everyone can blossom.

Minford quotes a passage from *New Tales of the World* (Liu Yiqing, China, fourth century AD), describing the bond between members of the Seven Sages of the Bamboo Grove as "stronger than bronze and fragrant as orchids". Fellowship connects the aspirations of people. The true gentleman's first goal is to be steadfast, and in this one may need to stand alone, but opportunities for fellowship will naturally arise.

A while ago I went on a trip to Tasmania, and I visited a small town in the midlands called Oatlands. I was looking for traces of my great great grandmother, Sarah Crosby, an Irish girl, a convict. I knew she had been sent to Oatlands in 1850. Given that she was Irish, I visited the Roman Catholic church. I met a priest who was staying there, who told me that he was not the parish priest. Rather, he was staying there as a hermit.

This was the first time I had ever met an avowed hermit, and I wondered if he would resent talking to me. But he didn't. We talked for an hour and a half, about Sarah and her life as a convict, and about modern life and religion. It was a rich exchange, even though our viewpoints were quite different (or somewhat different: one wonders). After one learns to be steadfast, opportunities for fellowship naturally arise. (Who was the hermit, the priest or myself?)

The second hexagram of this reading was another surprise: 55: Abundance. The trigrams are Thunder above Fire. Thunder is active and Fire is bright. It is a hexagram related to harvesting. The character is the king, and he stands like the sun at noon, to illuminate all under heaven. It is to remind us that there are good times; there will be moments when one is accepted and recognised, there are times when we can act with a free hand, unobstructed.

However, the structure of the situation contains its own caution. The sun only stays at its zenith for a short time, then there is decline. One must not expect moments of prominence or ease to last forever. The world is made up of waxing and waning, like the moon in its monthly cycle, or like the earth turning around the sun and giving us the seasons. As it is with the seasons, so it is with the affairs of humans.

Progress and success are possible, despite obstacles. This is a truth. But also, we serve our longer-term interests best if we keep correctness in the forefront of our minds. The idea of thriving is predicated on the foundation of steadfastness.

41 Thoughts about the stroke and healing

I finished reading the Norman Doidge book about the brain healing itself. Although the stories cross a very wide spectrum, for example, many of the stories are about babies in difficulty and some are about diseases like Parkinson's disease, there is a consistent theme that when something in the brain is not working, it will try to find other ways of accomplishing the same tasks. And, the corollary, that there are numerous ways that can help the brain along this path.

I could read the book again and look for specifics that I could consider applying to myself, but then I came across another book. I went to another book fair last week, and I found another book about the brain in trouble: David Roland's book, *How I Rescued My Brain* (2014). It seemed that this was my time for reading books about the brain.

Having started that book, about halfway through I saw that he referred to Norman Doidge's first book, so the ground is becoming familiar. He also mentioned Rita Carter, and I have two of her books. I used *Mapping the Mind* (1998) when I was writing my first book on ethics and values in 2008. There is a lot of reading, and re-reading, to do.

I am curious about what my brain has been doing over the past month or so, since the headache on 5th November. I don't want to put too much weight on the idea that I have had a stroke, but that is what I am being told by medical practitioners (plural) so, although I still find it puzzling, in stating that I have had a stroke, I am simply accepting the label for now.

I realised that I had two sorts of records of my daily activity. First, I have been writing this book, and I have kept a record of how many words I wrote each day (there is humour in this). Second, I use the I Ching each day, and I write notes on the hexagrams, usually up to one page of notes.

So, I could list all the dates from the beginning of November, and show the number of words written each day, and also the number of lines I wrote in my I Ching journal. I could also add the days on which I had medical appointments. Then I could examine it all to see if there were patterns that could be explained by the medical incident.

What I found was that there were patterns, although the meaning was not crystal clear. The baseline is established by knowing what I was doing in the first place. In November, I have often sat down to write a book in one month, of at least 50,000 words. This is the structure of "National Novel Writing Month" ("Nanowrimo"), a worldwide online event which attracts over 100,000 participants each year. It is not a competition; it is simply a whimsical structure to give would-be novelists a space in which they can focus.

I have participated in this event about eight times previously. I do it in a solitary way. I don't participate in any face-to-face gatherings. I simply record the number of words I have written each day on the website. For me it is a self-imposed structure that gets me to immerse myself in the task of writing a book, writing regularly each day. (You can work out how many words you would have to write each day to accumulate 50,000 by the end of the month.)

The daily "requirement" is quite comfortable for me. It is a pace that enables me to think and write in a relaxed but concentrated way. Each day, I have time to read through what I wrote the day before and then continue. There is not the time to review or rethink the whole story, and this is a good thing. It means you keep the flow going.

In my case, the work is never fiction. And I am not aiming to finish a book in the month; it just gets me well into it. By the end of the month, something is taking shape, and then I can continue afterwards, and review what I have done. I have completed many books from this beginning.

This account of Nanowrimo explains my mindset at the start of November. It was a familiar exercise for me, so it was comfortable. The only issue – and it was a major issue – was that I had never seen myself writing a book about the I Ching. So, there was internal resistance. Usually there is no internal resistance; I am generally working on something that I am keen to see happen. For example, if it is family history, it is a story that I am keen to tell, and it is a story that has not been known to anyone; I have uncovered it.

I started on 30th October (because I felt like it, and I make my own rules), writing 1,400 words. I worked for two hours, so I was not considering long sessions. It was also a measure of my reticence about the project. On 31st October, I spent longer at it: four hours, and I wrote 3,400 words. This meant I had found a thread, and I wanted to express the thought.

Over the next few days, I was thinking/writing for three or four hours per day, and I wrote 1,500 to 2,500 words per day. This was satisfying. I had one day off because I went to the city and had lunch with a friend. By Monday 4th November, I had written just over 10,000 words. This might suggest that I was confidently underway, but I don't think that was the case.

I think I felt that I had made a start, but I still didn't have a direction, and I didn't have a sense of what the whole of the book would be like. So, I think I felt that I could still be heading for failure, like driving headlong towards a cliff. Suddenly I would realise there was no more road. The train of thought will have evaporated. So, there would be no book; there would be nothing more of any value that I could see to write. Then I would tumble over the cliff.

Then there was Tuesday 5th November: a headache that lasted all day; most unusual, but I still thought I was finding a theme for the book, so I stayed at the computer for three hours. The result? Just 580 words. Disturbing.

However, the next two days I spent three or four hours each day at work, and I wrote around 2,200 words per day. It seemed to be moving along. Things seemed normal, although it felt as if a headache was hovering, not too far away. And then: nothing for the next three days. There was some trouble with my right eye, fuzziness and distortion in the middle of the visual field. My left eye was fine. This was severely interfering with my ability to read. This was the most disturbing thing. Reading is fundamental to my life.

Going back to 5th November: I threw the I Ching coins and got 21: Biting Through, with no moving lines. Normally I would have read Richard Rudd (because there were no moving lines) and written notes, but I wrote nothing. However, the message for the day was simple: it is as if there is an obstruction in the mouth, and the only way through is to bite through. It was a metaphor, but what it meant was to persevere and persist. All day, I felt that I had to resist, that that was the right thing to do – biting through.

Interestingly, I got the same hexagram on 8th November, this time with moving lines. I read another commentary this time, R.L. Wing, and she said, "Food cannot be nourished". My translation of that was: "Thoughts cannot be processed". I was waiting for things to become clear again.

The second hexagram was 58: Joyous: Lake doubled. It was good to have that positive image, beautiful, peaceful. And I took it to mean, possible.

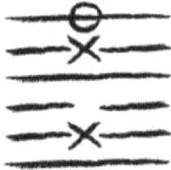

21: Biting Through: Shi He   58: Joyous/Lake: Dui

Over the next few days, I did the I Ching, and wrote down the hexagram or hexagrams, but I wrote no notes at all. These were the days on which I did no writing either. I felt that my head was slowly clearing, but the problem with my eye persisted.

Between Monday 11th November and Thursday 14th I was engaged with doctors: going to the eye doctor, the neurologists and having tests and scans done. On 13th I had the MRI scan and was told I had had a slight stroke and there was damage in my brain: bleeding. But

I have none of the impairments one associates with stroke, apart from the period of sluggishness.

So, I was foggy for a while, an indication being that when I went to have the MRI scan, I took the bus, then walked 200 metres to the place. I had not been there before; I just had the address. And I walked straight past it and didn't see it. I had to ring them up and ask for directions; I was further down the road. Since then, I have been past it on the bus, and it is incredibly well sign-posted: the name in large letters, all in bright colours. How could I have missed it? I was certainly impaired on that day.

On Friday 15th November, I wrote 2,700 words, a good day in my writing world. It was the first day of writing in over a week. On Saturday 16th I wrote 1,100 words, but the next week was patchy in terms of writing. There was one day when I saw a neurologist at the hospital.

By this time, I had recommenced writing in my I Ching journal. My head felt clearer, without a headache threatening. I was making progress in my reading of the books about the brain as well. The stories were harrowing, but the breakthroughs of the people were heartening, and there might be clues for me in it all.

I also have to consider the possibility that the yoga sessions that I do every day, in addition to the two classes per week, contributed to my lack of ongoing stroke symptoms. Perhaps I have had what people would call "a good recovery".

42 The I Ching and healing

In the books on the brain that I am reading, there are methods and approaches that were being suggested as a way of healing. And I am sure there is a whole world of books out there that advocate one approach or another. It's that kind of world: business, marketing, ideas and advertising. Bold claims. I am not against it all. Well, perhaps that's exactly what I am.

I don't want to be sucked into a vortex of cheerful certitude. In that world, it wouldn't matter if it was stroke, cancer, depression, heart troubles, bad digestion, or something else. There is a path to follow that involves following someone's instructions, and it probably involves the consumption of some kind of substance. I don't want to be caught up in disparaging people, but I do want to continue to live my own life ("Let your food be your medicine, and your medicine be your food").

Also, the first declaration I wish to make is that there is no point talking about healing unless you first accept that you are going to die one day. We are mortal. Any discussion of healing that seems to be based on the idea that you will never die is badly constructed. This is a good test. It seems to weed out some people with bold claims. It seems to puncture a fantasy.

My second declaration is that I have had a good life. My mother said this very late in life, ninety-three at the time. She had fallen and broken her femur, and I arrived at the hospital (ten hours' drive away) just as she emerged from the operating theatre on a stretcher, after the operation. She opened her eyes, saw me, and said, groggily, "You know, I've had a good life." I thought that was quite wonderful, and I told that story at her funeral six months later.

Similarly, I would say, at this point in time, aged seventy-four, "I have had a good life."

Now we can talk about healing.

Since the I Ching has been part of my life for such a long time, if there is to be healing, I want the I Ching to be part of my healing. Accordingly, I was bold. I asked the I Ching directly, "What would you tell me about the I Ching as the Way?" I meant this in the way that the *Tao Te Ching* means it, as a way to live one's life.

I know one should be cautious about asking bold questions, because the I Ching will not stand for pretentious nonsense and grandstanding. But I needn't have worried. The I Ching gave me a hexagram with no moving lines: 63: After Completion: Ji Ji. The hexagram is made up of Water above Fire. Think of a kettle of water boiling on a fire to make a cup of tea. A perfect moment.

63 and 64 are the last two hexagrams in the I Ching. 64 is Before Completion: that's another story, about why they are in this order. Because there were no moving lines, I resorted to Richard Rudd's book. It's a good thing that I don't throw hexagrams with no moving lines very often, because what he says is often overwhelming. It is such a vast point of view. Sometimes I think, I am not ready to read this.

The commentary opened with the statement: "The I Ching is an encyclopedia of consciousness that can only be accessed in a random manner." The issue I am facing is very much about my consciousness, and my approach to the I Ching is most definitely based on its principles of randomness. This is the pathway; not a logical method with defined steps, but an acceptance of its often strange perspective, accepting that there is wisdom in it each time I throw the coins.

The discussion Rudd offers concerns the characteristics of the two Gene Keys, 63 and 64. 63 is about logic; 64 is about imagination. 63 gives us the Shadow of Doubt; 64 gives us the Shadow of Confusion. There is great value in Doubt. It drives our advances in science, technology and other spheres. But as a personal presence, doubt never goes away. The mind craves certainty, and the only way the world offers certainty is in dogma, convention, and narrow-mindedness.

The function of Doubt is to drive us towards inquiry, which in turn leads us towards truth. But at a personal level we often end up not trusting ourselves, and distrusting others. When we fail to trust ourselves, we are unable to be creative. The Gift of Inquiry leads us to deeper levels of understanding and creativity. But through the journey, we realise we are bound up with what we are observing.

We cannot conduct this journey without accepting that we cannot do it as an objective observer; we are implicated. It leads us to the self, and who we are. This can feel threatening if we have doubts about ourselves. We may feel that we are a failure, and this is an impasse that logic cannot move beyond. Rudd says words to the effect that our endeavours are useless; we cannot conquer life, but then, Truth is everywhere. However, we must surrender to this.

This is strong stuff. We live in the midst of circumstances. We make choices in how we will live, and we are also constrained. Often, the "correct" course seems self-destructive. What are we to do? Or, in my case, why did the stroke happen to me? And, what is my best path forward from this point?

Rudd's last comment in this passage about 63 is: "Truth is everywhere. Give yourself a rest from worrying. Remember." It seems as though his last comment is the first step.

Is this a practical response to a person who has recently had "a slight stroke"? I accept that it is so. Nevertheless, I may find what Wilhelm has to say about this hexagram helpful.

Wilhelm says here, everything is in its proper place. The transition from confusion to order is complete. But, it is just when everything is in place that we need to exercise caution. Things might easily revert to disorder. I think, "Have I made a good recovery?" Is this what it means, that everything is in its correct place?

Wilhelm says, "The transition from the old to the new time is already accomplished." However, "we must be careful to maintain the right attitude." The wise person takes care of details, not being indifferent or careless. We are in a position to avoid a collapse into disorder.

Wilhelm comes back to the image of the kettle over the fire. Water and fire always contend with one another. We are a balance of fire and water, and we must be careful. The water can boil over and put out the fire. Or the fire can be too hot, and boil the water dry, Only the sage recognises when there is danger, and knows the balance that must be kept.

So, what I have is imagery. It doesn't seem much. But, I remember a friend who had a severe case of meningitis as an adult. It was a crisis, and he was not expected to live. He could not communicate, but he was still conscious, and aware of his situation. He decided that he had to help himself to recover.

What he found was a great source of strength was visualisation. He created specific images of himself on the way to recovery, and he held them in his mind while he slowly recovered physically, and likewise recovered his capacity to communicate. At some point he could assure people that he was conscious, sane, and intent on living with all his capacities. He made a complete recovery, to the amazement of his doctors, friends and family.

I do not disparage the power of images.

In an old book on yoga that I have (Segesman, 1973), visualisation is described as a conversation with our subconscious. The author says we can instruct the subconscious if our orders are clear, simple, and accompanied by deep feeling. But words are of no value; we must visualise what we want. Words are like speaking to a child in a foreign language. We need to hold the image in our mind so that it makes a clear impression on the subconscious.

43 The meaning of healing

Another day, I asked the I Ching: "What does 'healing' mean?" I used Stephen Karcher as the commentary. I received 29: Abyss: Kan, changing to 53: Developing Gradually: Jian. In broad brush strokes, this made sense. One had to go with the river, trusting that if you do, you will eventually emerge whole. And overall, one has to accept the pace of things, not expecting miracles overnight. You will develop gradually, so long as your intention is to develop.

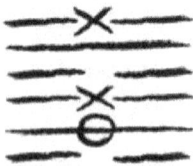

29: Abyss: Kan   53: Developing Gradually: Jian

Karcher says: Rise to the challenge. Use the energy of the pit. This is a critical moment that requires courage and determination. Connection to the spirits will carry you through. Importantly, for me, he adds: "Train yourself to confront this".

In the moving lines, there are warnings: What is coming is more than you can handle; pull back. And, losing the way; trapped for three years. But, there was also this line: a pit with sheer sides. Do not leave the inner centre. Seek through the small. Be flexible and modest.

Now, a few weeks after the incident, although I feel okay, and I am functioning "normally", going about my usual business each day (and I am writing smoothly), when I think about the state of my brain, it leaves me to wonder. If a dark moment was approaching, would I be able to see it? Would I be able to prevent it? The image of a pit with sheer sides is pertinent. Karcher's advice would be: I should not aim for a final conquest over my brain. I should keep to the inner centre, and "seek through the small".

I take this to mean, live moment by moment, watch my thoughts, not allow dark thoughts to take me over, and be aware, and let go of worry. I think I am at a point in my life where the overt negative thoughts have receded, but there is still a shadow lurking, which I would call "the shadow of negative thoughts" that still puts my body and mind into a low state of constant tension. But it is something I can work on.

What does Karcher say about 53? He calls it "Gradual Advance". It is a particular type of change: regular development that proceeds in stages. It is moving towards union. It is part of the fundamental process of change. One of its images is about harvesting. The trigrams are Wind above Mountain. The wind in the I Ching is mostly a gentle breeze. It penetrates everything. It is steady and subtle, and it signifies a connection with spirit. Karcher says, move with yin energy and you will achieve mastery; you will acquire a new field of activity.

This is very positive when I apply it to the idea of healing. I find it very applicable.

149

More recently, I threw the I Ching coins, still thinking about healing but not wanting to be repetitive, and I obtained two hexagrams: 9: Taming Power of the Small: Xiao Xu, changing to 29: Abyss: Kan. So, this was picking up on Karcher's comment: "seek through the small", and it brings me back to the image of the ravine or gorge.

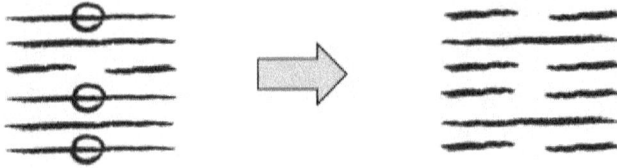

9: Taming Power of the Small: Xiao Xu

29: Abyss: Kan

I am reading Huang. Hexagram 9 is the idea of a person accumulating nourishment but not yet being strong enough for great pursuits. There are dense clouds but no rain yet. Nevertheless, the time is prosperous and smooth. There is one yin line in among five yang lines. It is in the fourth position. This is the place of the minister who carries out the administration of the kingdom. The ruler is in the fifth place. As a yin line it is gentle, but it is also capable. It leads through gentleness.

This seems to refer to managing and carrying out practical tasks, like focusing on what I need to change about my mental state. At this time there is a slowdown in progress, but this is fine. It is not a problem or an obstacle. In the end, one's will will be fulfilled.

Then I come full circle; I am back in the pit. Huang says there is danger, but all is not lost. "Maintain your confidence, soothe your mind." One can pass through safely if one follows the way of heaven. Rely on heart-and-mind. He also says, water flows, it does not accumulate.

This means that one must always be in the moment, rather than thinking one has amassed sufficient knowledge and skills to put one in a permanently ruling position. One's heart is always beating, and

150

the world is what it is moment by moment. One must be here now, and trust that one can meet the moment gracefully. One does not have to meet all moments, just this one.

I am not in possession of a plan for combatting the threat of another stroke. Could I convince any medical practitioner that I have acquired the needful knowledge and instituted practical methodologies for protecting myself against such an attack?

I think that I am in the presence of paradox here, but I do wish to be careful about language. The I Ching is quite careful about language and the worlds it creates. I continue in the worlds it is giving me. Water flows, it does not accumulate. Deeds will be honoured. The taming power is in the small. And development is gradual.

44 Another journey into the past

In one of my journals (this one was in 2014) I found a passage about how to live well. Notes for my future self? Perhaps. It had occurred to me while reading a book on meditation that the book did not provide a context for this practice of meditation. It just said you should meditate, and talked about how to do that. My question was how this activity of meditation fitted into a person's life, and what else there should be in a person's life.

I thought about this broadly. I get most of my ideas from broad space. I thought, if you are going to tell someone how they should live, you should give them all the elements, and show how they fit together. Such didacticism needs context. It's not enough for the exercise advocate to say, you should exercise. Et cetera.

In my mind, the key ingredient is balance. What is a judicious mix? So, I proposed four ingredients of a balanced life:

1. Stillness, or meditation
2. Movement: this is physical movement, which could be exercise, yoga, dance, as well as activities or projects
3. "Changing the story": looking at your prevailing ideas and mental models, the ones that keep going round and round in your head, and asking whether they are healthy (for you), and being willing to change them
4. Love, gratitude and appreciation.

What is the right balance of these ingredients? My answer to this question was, it's a matter of personal judgement, asking yourself questions like: is this healthy? Could I do better?

And finally, I wrote, "How you answer these questions is what will define you."

As far as it goes, I still think this is a worthwhile statement, ten years later. Following this passage in the journal, there was an I Ching reading. It was a hexagram without any moving lines: 16: Enthusiasm: Yu. Appropriate, I think. It aligns with the statement, as it contains movement (Thunder above) and stillness (Earth below).

My notes say, "With this understanding, you can set armies in motion", in line with the second proposition: activities or projects. In response to the third proposition, my notes say, "Adapt yourself to the circumstances and follow the natural principles of life, leading confidently and meeting with enthusiasm."

And, in response to the fourth proposition, my notes say, "Act in such a way that you would invite the ancestors to be present."

In this period, I was having difficulty with my work environment, and I wanted to move. I had been working on a contract for three years and it was about to end. As a reflection of the difficulties I was experiencing, I was offered a short-term, five-month contract that would have ended the week before Christmas. In the context, I thought this was meant to be unkind, a form of punishment, and it could very likely leave me unemployed at a bad time of the year.

I decided I had to find another job. And another job did turn up, in a related organisation. I applied for it and I was successful. So, there was a day when I had to decide to accept the new position, and I was driving to the new place to talk to the new employer about it. Driving along the road, I was overtaken by a hearse carrying a coffin. I thought this was notable; I don't think I had ever been overtaken by a hearse in my entire life. It was the opposite of the usual, if infrequent occurrence, finding yourself overtaking a hearse.

The next day, I was in my car again, and I was driving to my old job to let them know that I would be leaving, not taking the short, punitive contract. I was overtaken by the same hearse, only this time it did not have a coffin in it. I thought, that was my old job: it was indeed dead, and it has been buried.

I consulted the I Ching at this time of change, and I received 64: Before Completion: Wei Ji. I read Stephen Karcher's book. It said: you are on the edge of a change; everything is possible. You are about to cross the river. A young fox crosses the water, taking care not to get its tail wet. Things are moving towards their proper place. Life cannot be exhausted.

There were many changes happening in this period. Apart from the job I had, I was working on another project which took a great deal of work and was uncertain of being successful in the market subsequently. I was also trying to keep my personal life and my home stable, and my finances healthy. One day I simply wrote, "I am a multitude of thoughts and feelings." Then I threw the coins.

I obtained two hexagrams: 58: Joyousness: Dui, followed by 16: Enthusiasm: Yu.

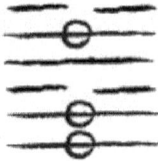

58: Joyousness: Dui   16: Enthusiasm: Yu

I thought, the I Ching is constantly trying to help me! For 58 I read: Accept the energy and allow it to stimulate you. The image is the joyous dancer. It is an encouragement to express yourself openly.

For 16 I read: you have great reserves of grace and power.

I noted, the I Ching does not make decisions for you. It simply suggests a fresh way to look at the issue. This time, it reminded me of what I needed to keep in mind. What you work on should be a joy, not a drudge. I decided to curtail the project; instead of three phases, I finished off the first phase and left it at that.

I was wrestling with big ideas, and using the I Ching to engage with them. I was thinking about the different kinds of philosophies one encounters in society. For example, one approach says you must decide on big goals for your life, and then pursue them with discipline and perseverance. Another approach says you should have no goals. Instead, you should be open and receptive, and respond to whatever presents itself.

I wondered whether the difference between the two was simply one's age; when you are young, it may be important to have goals, and as you get older it may be more important to be receptive.

The I Ching gave me 35: Progress: Jing, followed by 27: Nourishment: Yi.

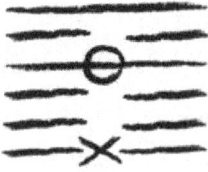

35: Progress: Jing   27: Nourishment: Yi

I read what one of my books had to say, then returned to the question. I felt that the I Ching did not say that one or the other approach was correct. I thought of Karl Marx's concept of the dialectic. It is not a question of eliminating one or the other, but learning how to hold them in dynamic tension.

Both of the approaches have validity, but there is potential conflict between them. It is our task to turn this into creative tension. We need to be aware of the constant flow between yin and yang. And, we need to remember, what is the end state we are striving towards after all these efforts?

I thought, it depends. Sometimes we are in pursuit of a goal and things are progressing smoothly. There are wise words that apply to such times: shine brightly (like the sun above the earth) and enjoy the moment. Remember to always act out of honour, thoughtfulness and kindness, to be forgiving of someone who may offend you. And, to exercise caution: observe the flow, and keep building your strength to face the difficulties that may come.

In the end, the goal has to be about more than your own success. It has to be about sustenance for both yourself and others. And you need to be moderate in your consumption and generous towards others. We are goal-oriented creatures, and we thrive when we are in pursuit of an honourable and challenging goal. But we must also see that we are complex creatures who are made up of more than goal-seeking behaviour. (There is doing and there is being.)

The healthy path is to have numerous goals that address different parts of ourselves. However, there is also part of us that is beyond goals. Goals are invariably specific, but ironically, they deliver us into the world of uncertainty, expending ourselves in pursuit of their fulfilment. And their fulfilment is likewise a specific, limited thing.

As with Marx's concept, we need to be a dialectic of goals and no-goals. We need to temper our goal-seeking with human values (eg honesty, consideration of others), and we need to recognise ourselves in our eternal, goal-free presence.

Another day, I asked the question, "How to be me from now on?"

The hexagram was a clear response: 7: Legion, Army or Multitude: Shi. There are five yin lines, and one yang line in the second place. This is the place of the local leader. This is to say, when there is one defined leader, there is order and progress. Otherwise, things can fall to pieces.

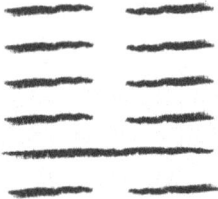

```
▬▬▬   ▬  ▬
▬▬▬   ▬  ▬
▬▬▬   ▬  ▬
▬▬▬   ▬  ▬
▬▬▬▬▬▬▬▬▬
▬▬▬   ▬  ▬
```

Accordingly, in personal life, one should have a defined direction, so as not to fall into chaos. The multitude gathers around the leader, which is: a clear idea about the kind of person you are. The trigrams are Water underneath Earth. Water is stored in the earth and it is available for use when needed (thus we have wells). Water stands for the emotions (in contrast to the intellect), and when it is stored in the earth, there is peace.

That was "how to be me from now on".

45 Another big question

The I Ching is remarkable in what it throws up in response to questions. This is a random process; who can predict what will ensue from two hands shaking three coins and then letting them fall onto the table? In my journal I was asking bold questions and doing this with confidence that the hexagrams would tell a story that would make sense.

The question I asked on one occasion was this: Should we focus on outward achievement or on inward development?

The response I got was indeed remarkable. The first hexagram was made up of the same trigram, repeated. It was 58: Lake/Joyous: Dui. There were two moving lines, in the second and fifth places. This meant that the hexagram changed to 51: Thunder/Shake: Zhen: another hexagram made up of a pair of repeated trigrams. The answer was as bold as the question.

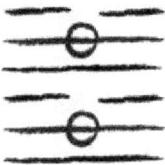

58: Lake/Joyous: Dui   51: Thunder/Shake: Zhen

The significance of doubled trigrams is that the outside and the inside of the person or situation are subject to the same conditions. In some hexagrams, the inside and the outside are at odds with each other. For example, in 12: Stagnation: Pi, the higher part of the person is striving to be spiritual, but the lower part, the body, is striving to go its own way, so there is great tension.

You could say it was ironic that the inside and outside are the same in the two hexagrams, since that was the very thrust of the question. The hexagrams were telling me, already, that it doesn't matter whether you focus on outward achievement or inner development. If you do it with integrity, the other will follow.

I could understand the first hexagram, Lake, as referring to the inner. The idea is, if you focus on inner development, enjoy what you are doing. Seek the joy and depth of the lake. Inner development should not be too serious or austere. And joy should express itself outwardly. It will lead to outward expression.

And the second hexagram, Thunder, I could understand as referring to outward achievement. The aim is to shake things up, to break through obstacles in the same way that thunder cuts through the tension in the air. And the message of Thunder is to keep your focus on the correct way of operating. Remain undisturbed inwardly and you will succeed in your endeavour.

(I have written about hexagrams with doubled trigrams earlier. Lake is in Chapter 24 and Thunder is in Chapter 22.)

46 The great knowledge

In the same journal I expressed the idea that there is a "Great Knowledge" out there, the knowledge of all things in the universe. You can think of it as a thing that exists. In the *Tao Te Ching*, it talks about the "Great Unknowing", but what I am thinking of is the opposite of that. It is the aggregation of all knowing of all the different kinds of things. Then I asked the I Ching for its perspective on this idea.

The I Ching gave me 28: Great Exceeding: Da Guo, changing to 62: Little Exceeding: Xiao Guo. This was an apt pairing, I thought: two kinds of excess. In 28, the ridgepole of a house is under a great burden and it is sagging. Lake is above Wind: four yang lines are on the inside, and there are yin lines at the top and bottom.

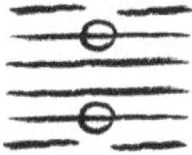

28: Great Exceeding:
Da Guo

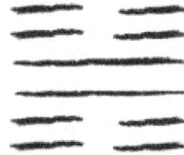

62: Little Exceeding:
Xiao Guo

In consulting the I Ching, one has to consider, where do I stand in relation to the question? My first thought was, the Great is excessive. The hexagram contains the concept that one follows along with an idea (Wind is below) and allows it to come to expression (Lake/joy is above), but the result is problematic. One needs to have somewhere to go, and impose a direction on things. Accordingly, I think, perhaps the Great Knowledge is not a helpful concept. Does it end up becoming like a great burden on the roof of a house, causing the ridgepole to sag?

Why would this be? I think it is because the Great Knowledge comes to be seen as static and inflexible and it imposes on us, and this is not the nature of most knowledge. Knowledge generally lives in a dynamic realm. For example, the idea that all of the universe exists as atoms was considered to be knowledge for over a hundred years, but then it was discovered that atoms were not indivisible units. They had parts within them: electrons, protons and so on.

To think about the nature of knowledge, one should consider early maps of the world and how they showed Australia. In maps of the 1600s, only tiny parts of the Australian coastline had been mapped; the rest was completely blank. In 1803, Matthew Flinders and George Bass circumnavigated Australia for the first time and mapped the entire coastline, travelling in a small boat and accompanied by a cat. But, even given current maps, one has to consider the changes that occur over time. Knowledge is a conditional concept.

Pushing this idea further, I think that there are different kinds of knowledge. Knowledge about people and their nature is not always reducible to quantifiable "facts". To treat everything the same way is what creates the burden that weighs the roof down.

What then, of the second hexagram? Here, Thunder is above Mountain. There are four yin lines on the outside, and two yang lines within, hence, the small preponderates: Little Exceeding. The lines look like the body of a bird in the middle (the two yang lines), with the outer yin lines as its wings. I read: it is better for the bird to fly low rather than flying high and being caught in a storm.

It is still safe for the bird if it follows proper conduct. Indeed, there is great good fortune. Small things may be done, but not great things. Another meaning of the hexagram is that a person in a position of authority whose capabilities are limited should exercise caution in the role.

I conclude that the Great Knowledge is real, but it is like a great storm that a small bird may fly into and come to harm if it is not careful. I think that beyond the Great Knowledge there is the Great Knowing, where the emphasis has shifted from the knowledge to the knower: who is it who knows? For me, that means, who is it who learns? It is the activity of learning that is important.

In the second hexagram, the one who learns is not the king, the ruler, or someone powerful. It is the small bird. Moreover, the small bird is a creature that is aware of danger. And yet, there is still optimism: the bird still flies, and it still makes the crossing. There is humility in this, as well as bravery. This is an interesting destination for a thought-play on knowledge.

Lastly, I remember the *Tao Te Ching* and the Great Unknowing. Perhaps the truth is, to see the Great Knowing as an amassed possession of humans and a sign of our dominance, is probably a mere conceit. The Tao tells us that beyond us is not terrain that can be conquered, but the vast unknowing. In the face of it, humility would serve us better.

47 Considering this project

I have blundered along this far, and I seem to be committed. It is time to ask the I Ching what it thinks of what I am doing. I give it the title: "A Singular Book of Great Esteem" and ask the question.

I obtain a single hexagram; there are no moving lines. And it is 35: Progress: Jing.

Hence, I read Richard Rudd's wild book about gene keys. He always starts with the broad situation of humans: the shadows we live under. We live in hunger; we are always striving towards something. And we are prone to externalising that hunger: rather than working on ourselves, we create technology. We change the outer world.

The irony is that our efforts in the outer world pull us away from our inner natural rhythm. Then we experience a range of negative emotions, and we look for an effective external soother, or a distraction. Then we become addicted to it. Alternatively, we experience disappointment.

How does the I Ching fit into this scenario? It is the means by which we can explore our inward world. Rudd describes the Gift of this hexagram (or gene key) as Love. It releases us from the hunger, and it enables us to embark on an adventure. The exploration of the I Ching and its hexagrams is an adventure.

Rudd says that this changes the chemical balance in our bodies. It activates tryptophan, which is connected to secretion of serotonin, the chemical which makes us feel good. But he also says that it is not as simple as that; the changes involve many chemicals, and the result is a delicate balance of all of them.

Rudd says the 35th gene key is unique among all the sixty-four gene keys, in that it stands alone. All the other gene keys are in various combinations called codon rings. Each gene key combines with one or more other gene keys to create a field of evolutionary activity. It may deal with light, water, humanity, illusion, destiny and so on. The 35th gene key gives us a direct choice in how our reality is constructed. Here we give expression to our free will. Our spirit can break free.

It would appear that the I Ching regards itself as a great vehicle for inner development. The Gift of the 35th gene key is to raise our awareness through the recognition of love. It is a leap out of fear to see the world the way it does. You come to trust the universe and what is happening around you. It is okay; there is a pathway through for you. In some translations of the I Ching, 35 is called "Easy Progress".

When Rudd discusses the Siddhi level, he uses the word "Boundlessness". Humanity is in the midst of evolution, going back billions of years. In this sense we are progressing slowly, and despite the immense difficulties of life today, the evolutionary progress continues. But it is as if the 35th gene key is a secret within that plan. It opens up the field of boundlessness.

Rudd says, ponder on the concept of boundlessness in your daily life. You will move out of your mind (your cognitive faculty) and into your heart. You will see yourself as part of the infinite, and your life will embody infinite possibilities.

My view: the I Ching works with us day by day, or as often as we find it possible to consult it. It becomes a familiar, wise friend. We each face a myriad of circumstances, and we are a mixture of strong and weak, vision and blind spots, capacity to love and feelings of overwhelm. In Progress, the sun rises above the earth. Wilhelm says, "The superior man brightens his bright virtue."

48 The monk and the ordinary life

I have never sought to be a monk who lives separately from the ordinary life of the world. I have felt that what I need to learn in this life I must learn as an ordinary citizen, earning a living, exercising a skill, and engaging in ordinary relationships. I saw the monk as a person who has a daily routine and who seeks to be centred, but who is living separate from the busy world. The ordinary person faces different issues every day and has to try different ways and eradicate habits that deaden the mind.

The notes I wrote about the monk were on the last page of the journal I have been perusing. Perhaps today I would express the issue differently, but that was how I phrased the context for my question at the time: Which is preferable: the monk or the ordinary man? (I mean "person", but the rhythm of "man" is better here.)

Sometimes I think, in retrospect, that the I Ching could have been harsher with me. It could have been scathing about the shallowness of my understanding. Yet I could see in its response that it was trying to teach me. It gave me 32: Duration: Heng (Thunder above Wind), with moving lines. The following hexagram was 57: Gentle Penetration: Xun (Wind upon Wind).

32: Duration: Heng   57: Gentle Penetration: Xun

How did I interpret this? I wrote: each time I throw the coins, I throw them in the same way, but each time the result is unique. The purpose of one's daily actions is duration, and the secret of duration is relationship. The model for this is the marriage between man and wife.

Accordingly, both the habits of a monk and the acceptance of the challenge of new experiences are valid. In both cases, the appropriate attitude is to be alive to the present. And, the goal is to learn the distinction between what is lasting and what is evanescent.

The two pertinent instructions are: 1) to be steadfast and upright, and 2) to have somewhere to go. The firm (Thunder) is above, the gentle (Wind) is below. The sage stands firm without changing his/her aim.

The moving lines (three of them) concern keeping the balance between firmness and docility, and also, avoiding descending into a state of constant agitation.

57: Gentle Penetration (Wind doubled) means that wind is above and below. Whether one is a monk or an ordinary person, one is a traveller in this world. Proceed humbly to the central and correct position. Then your will may be fulfilled without any violation of the spirit of the Way.

Our society leans towards dramatic gestures and aggressive action. It is transforming to consider that this is not the way of Tao. In other words, that is not the true way of the universe. To attain Duration, one must follow the way of the universe.

It may seem that these are merely "flowery" words, but in contemplating these words, one's mind is gradually transformed. (I did not write this in the journal (2017); this is what I have come to think now (2024).)

49 Coming back again (Returning)

Often, it will seem that the message that comes through the hexagram(s) is the final message; it is the last thing you need to hear. From this point, one can go forth and live one's life, holding to that message steadily. But circumstances change, even from day to day, and the message of the I Ching changes also. It seems that it is nudging you incrementally towards your goal.

It is like having a diamond in your hand, and you turn it over and over, and you keep seeing new facets of it (not that I have ever had a diamond in my hand!). Let's say I have been in the strange space of feeling okay, but there has been an event that suggests that I was not okay. And have I really been feeling okay? Doesn't the event suggest that I was not okay, in some significant respect?

I attempt to address this thought. Let's say that, when I had the big headache, I had allowed something to oppress me. It was subtle but real. I felt that I was not capable of creating the book I had embarked on. This meant that every moment of my efforts was taking me closer to a point of collision, where my inadequacy would become obvious and dramatically disillusioning. It was a pressure, squeezing my brain. And, of course, getting sick is a way of avoiding the situation: I wouldn't be able to finish the book if I was sick.

Now the I Ching says to me: 55: Abundance: Feng, with one moving line, so the hexagram changes to 34: Great Strength: Da Zhuang. I read what Stephen Karcher says: "Abounding means there were many previous grounds for sorrow. The new king receives the mandate. He becomes great."

55: Abundance: Feng

34: Great Strength: Da Zhuang

I think: if I learn how, I can disengage from the mindset that led to the headache. Karcher tells the story of King Wen being in the mourning hut because his father had died, but the corrupt Shang emperor was making conditions for the people worse. Action against him was needed. One day, there was a solar eclipse, and the sky became dark at midday. He decided that this was an omen, and he should abandon mourning and go to battle.

He accepted the responsibility of the moment and donned his armour to go to war. His truly shocking action was to take his father's coffin, hoisted on the shoulders of the soldiers, and carry it into battle with them. It was such a dramatic and unprecedented action that the soldiers were galvanised and were victorious.

Accordingly, the I Ching is saying to me: this is not a time for mourning. You are capable of a fundamental change. Be exuberant. In the moving line it says: The connection to spirit will carry you through.

This is followed by 34, which says this is a time of invigorating strength. Drive on. As with soldiers, there may be injuries and wounds, but you are to take to the field. Coming out of seclusion and proceeding in strength lets you look into the heart of Heaven and

Earth. Continually correct your path. Break through established conventions. A new cycle is beginning. Disengage from the past.

And that could, indeed, be the last message from the I Ching: encouraging, inspiring.

But, of course, it is not. Days follow days, and the days differ. One keeps turning the diamond in one's hand over and over. It is between Christmas and New Year, and the time seems quiet, even still. Most of the stories about the year have been dismal. The atmosphere in which many people work today is hapless and nasty, and even ordinary "good" people act badly. They do not act like managers whose job is transformation.

I have a clear idea about this. Most people work in organisations, and there are many levels in organisations. At each level, issues will arise, and the point of managers is to resolve the tensions that occur at their level, through intelligence and diplomacy. However, poor managers do not do this. Instead, they simply transfer the pressure downwards, enforcing demands from above that are mindless and, sometimes, unreal, and even impossible.

For example, the higher management want more productivity, so they demand it. There is an order sent downwards. An intelligent lower manager will consider what is really possible, solve real problems, and mediate the messages both ways, up and down. Thus, transformation occurs! A poor manager does none of this; they add no value whatsoever in their role.

Most of the stories I have heard this year have been dismal: poor managers, incompetent workers, and employees giving up quietly.

These are days of quiet, but it is simply respite. I am no longer part of the warfare, but I hear about it, at close quarters. There needs to be a fresh spirit, that comes from a renewing force, not from despair and flatness.

The I Ching, on one of these days, says 51: Arousing: Zhen, followed by 24: Returning: Fu.

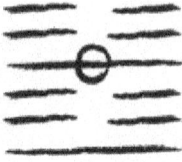

51: Arousing: Zhen   24: Returning: Fu

Wilhelm describes this as the elder son seizing rule with energy and power. It is violent; it arouses terror. But the shock brings success. Wilhelm's words are striking: "Shock comes – oh, oh! Then laughing words – ah, ah! It terrifies the people for miles around, but the sage does not let a single drop fall from the sacrificial spoon and ladle. He is composed in spirit. The superior man sets his life in order, and has reverence."

I seldom see I Ching readings from a social or political point of view. I usually consider what it means at a personal level. How should I approach the circumstances of my life, which leads to what stance should I take, and what action should I take? I might feel dismayed, vicariously, by the stories of my compatriots (family and friends). I could offer advice, but lacking context, my advice might be inappropriate and ineffectual.

Instead, I talk about my own experiences of difficult situations, and talk about what I think of the effects of those actions, what I think about those actions now, and what I would do differently. I don't pretend to understand all the factors they are affected by. But the actions of "the older son" indicate that sometimes a new broom is needed, and it is appropriate to act boldly.

And one has to learn the calm heart of the sage. The single moving line I got was a puzzle: nine in the fourth place. "Shock is mired." Here, movement within the mind is crippled. (I could relate to that.)

If one is neither resisting a force nor yielding to enable victory, one can become stuck. The circumstances are difficult.

I thought I should pay attention to this odd comment. It is about the mind, and it suggests that resisting a force can be healthy, and so can yielding (judiciously), but if one is undecided (or in a dither), that is not so healthy.

One normally thinks of thunder as breaking through recalcitrant situations and bringing, or enabling, the new. But even here there can be complications.

Yet, the hexagram changes to 24: Fu. It is a matter of persevering. Returning is a powerful image in the I Ching. The image is that all the yang forces have been expelled, so one is without strength, but then a single firm line re-enters from below. There is a journey through the I Ching, following all the hexagrams in their current sequence; 23, the hexagram that comes before 24, is about corruption. Returning is the beginning of the rebuilding; it is a new cycle.

The time of darkness is over. Whereas in 55 there was a solar eclipse to mark a significant point in time, 24 signifies a seasonal change: it is the solstice. There is a free flow of energy, spontaneous and easy. The old goes and the new is introduced. Importantly, there is no selfishness and there are no mistakes.

Wilhelm's story from the ancient times is that at the time of the solstice, the kings closed the passes and people did not travel. He comments that energy that is renewing itself must be treated tenderly and with care at the beginning, so that the return will lead to flowering. He mentions that this is true of recovery after an illness.

The image that stays with me is that natural energy is precipitating a seasonal change. It is not as if I have to force it. I just need to go with it. I need to be observant of energy, observant of it in order to understand what is happening. I need to trust it. When the ancient king closed the passes, it was not out of weakness or fear; it was to give time to energy to renew itself, and this was a natural process.

50 Another perspective on progress

A while after I received the hexagram 35: Progress: Jing, I received the hexagram again, but with a twist. This time, I received hexagram 23 first, and it changed to 35. 23 is Splitting Apart: Bo. Here, Mountain is above Earth: it is too high above its foundation, and it is unstable. Mountain and Earth are splitting apart. Hua-Ching Ni calls it Erosion.

23: Splitting Apart: Bo   35: Progress: Jing

Alfred Huang calls it Falling Away, and uses the image of a landslide. If you look at the lines, there is a single yang line at the top and five yin lines below. They are rising, seeking to banish the yang line. "The little fellows are extending their power." I wonder, is this a reference to the stroke? Who are the "little fellows"?

They could be bad habits of mind, or a call to me that I need to raise my awareness and refine my practices. The instruction that Huang offers is to be still, and to contemplate the yin and yang of increase and decrease: the cycle.

However, it is not a call to harsh discipline. One is asked to be benevolent to those below us; in this case, one's own body and thoughts. Huang says, build the house anew, on a solid foundation.

The single moving line indicates that calamity was near at hand. Okay.

This time, with 35: Progress, it is Huang's voice I hear. We are to build the house anew, but it is a favourable start. Brightness appears above the earth, and the submissive (Earth) aligns with the bright (Fire). Lord Kang is honoured with gifts of horses, and he is received at the royal court three times in one day (one remembers not to be too literal in such matters).

It is the gentle who advances, not the aggressive. One remembers that this alludes to two different mindsets; it is not simply a switch of technique. The difference is on the inside. The king maintains his country in order, and the superior person cultivates his/her virtue.

Could it be that inner changes must occur, not external shifts? And could it be that the inner changes are not about harder discipline, but more awareness, and more trust in the universe. Our efforts to find harmony are constantly diverted into the outer world. It can be subtle, like trusting pills to fix us, or an outer regime or practice. These "inner" practices are soon outer routines, and as such, they still pull us away from our inner natural rhythm.

I think it takes much practice to be aware of all our emotions, and to stop automatically looking for external soothers. But in tandem with this, we must trust the universe, which is to say, "Right now (at this moment), everything is okay. I am okay."

This is to trust the Tao, which is the spirit of everything, and its movement, the increase and the decrease, like breath, in and out. And kindness is at its heart. This is why the king keeps the country in order, because he embodies justice and kindness. He evokes the love of the people.

Gradually, a single vision emerges from the sixty-four hexagrams. In any hexagram, one sees all of the hexagrams.

51 The young person's quest for a mask

When I was young, I felt that I had to contrive a mask that I could wear that would enable me to fit in, to be accepted by others, both a set of friends and the wider society. It was not as simple as that; there were elements of inner striving as well, to learn all manner of things, and to express myself.

However, my overriding feeling was that I did not understand many things, not nearly enough, and I wanted to be accepted. I needed a mask. I don't feel this way now. Part of the change was that I realised that many other people did not know very much, and yet they survived. Another reason for the change was that I developed more confidence in myself.

I asked the I Ching for its thoughts. What it said was illuminating and, as it often is, surprising.

The first hexagram was 48: Well: Jing, changing to 28: Great Excess: Da Guo. Another name that is used for 48 is Replenishing. I figured the I Ching was saying that if one wants replenishment, one's focus needs to be inward, not external, that is, not on what other people want or how to please them. But what did Great Excess mean?

48: The Well: Jing   28: Great Excess: Da Guo

This time, I was reading Hua-Ching Ni, and sometimes he expresses things in exactly the way I need in order to see the hexagram's relevance to my situation. I am following through from the first hexagram, thinking, if one lives one's life outwardly, trying to develop a suitable mask to satisfy others, one will end up like this. The burden on the roof is too great and the roofbeam is sagging. The person is unbalanced and in imminent danger. Action must be taken immediately to correct the situation before destruction occurs.

The message of the Well is strong. The well always stays in the same place. The village and the people may move, but not the well. This is to say, people are fickle; they change their minds, or times change. One would not want to be reliant on that perspective. So, what is the well? Where does one find sustenance?

I don't think the I Ching answers that question. What it does say, however, is that the water is pure, and it is essential to life. Accordingly, one should apply that test to what one follows and what one devotes time to studying. Is this pursuit integral to life, or is it tawdry, demeaning, shallow, or unsatisfactory in some other way? The hexagram of the Well concentrates our attention on how we access the water.

We have to have a rope that is long enough to reach the water. We have to have a bucket that is in good condition. We have to keep the sides of the well in good condition. We have to make sure we are careful when we lower and raise the bucket. So, the water (knowledge, skills, opportunities) we seek to obtain must be worthy of our respect.

There may be another caution in the commentary too. The well is not concerned with gain or loss. It provides water to anyone who comes to the well. Keeping this in mind will save us from coming under the influence of people who only wish to exploit us.

The commentary on Great Excess goes further. Examining one's character, if one is aggressive or egotistical, this is akin to a sagging roofbeam. So, also, is the person who is too passive or fearful. Inner strength must be in balance with what is required externally.

What is required is the ability to walk in the central way. It is possible to learn what situations require, and act appropriately. The accomplished person does what is "just right", not too much and not less than enough. But to do this, one must have inner awareness. Trying to fit to the demands of a mask will not enable one to be "just right".

52 On a new day, without an agenda

There are some days when there are no pressing issues. It is as if one can decide for oneself today. You approach the I Ching and you have no urgent question that needs an answer. Would it be frivolous to throw the coins today? In my case, even the spectre of the stroke is at a distance.

On a day without an agenda, one yet needs to remind oneself of the vastness and the need for trueness. And one still exists within a milieu where one needs to contribute appropriately.

I obtained 30: Brightness: Li, which changed to 13: Seeking Harmony: Tong Ren. For 30, I would say, this is a time of light, and in that time one should articulate and spread the light. I am reading from Stephen Karcher. We should remember that Fire contends with Water, and thus there is an inner axis of change within the individual.

30: Brightness: Li

13: Seeking Harmony:
Tong Ren

With this understanding, one can create a place where people can congregate, because the bright omens reveal the spirits. Radiance works in the heart to bring the spark of life, and a quiet centre where one's voice can be heard. There is joy in this.

The moving line is in the fifth place, and it says the danger has passed. The spirits are appeased. A decisive encounter approaches, and you are assured of victory. People come together to join their power together, after a time of loneliness.

On a day without an agenda, Brightness, Radiance throws light on an open road towards joy, and it is joy in fellowship with others.

The second hexagram confirms this view. It means seeking harmony with other people. It is to share with them and unite people together in a task. Find places of agreement and develop a common understanding. Fire is below Heaven, which is interpreted as inner awareness transforming old powers and structures.

In Tong Ren, everyone gathers after the isolation of winter, and they step into the great stream in unity. This is a return to the original unity. We have known this; we remember it and welcome it again. Karcher refers to the spirits, which is to say, we do not feel alone in this experience. It is greater than our aloneness; it is even greater than our shared joy. We become capable of greatness. Note that the next hexagram in the sequence is 14: Great Being.

53 Yoga and the I Ching

I have practised yoga regularly for over twenty years, so I am aware when yoga is mentioned in a text. In hexagram 52: Keeping Still: Gen, Richard Wilhelm mentions yoga. It is not much; he is discussing how one achieves a quiet heart, and he says, "Possibly the words of the text embody directions for the practice of yoga."

The text says: "Keeping still. Keeping his back still so that he no longer feels his body. He goes into his courtyard and does not see his people. No blame."

John Minford mentions the fact that Wilhelm alludes to yoga, but he does not embellish. The other commentaries I have do not mention yoga, with only a couple of exceptions. The commentators generally talk of "keeping still" as referring to stilling the body and cultivating awareness.

Only Carol Anthony (1988) refers to yoga (in hexagram 52), which she describes as relaxation exercises preparatory to meditation. Stephen Karcher mentions yoga, but under the hexagram 20: Viewing: Guan. He mentions it in order to note that "guan" is the word used to translate "yoga". This makes sense, because yoga is a way of concentrating awareness on the body (guan means watching).

The lines in the hexagram start with the toes, then the calves, then the hips. After this there are the trunk and the jaws, and finally, there is "noble-hearted keeping still". If these are directions for yoga, they refer to the aspect of yoga that is concerned with quieting the body as a prelude to meditation.

Yoga is also concerned with movement, and sees the object of the practice as balance between movement and relaxation. Hexagrams 51 and 52 are a pair, representing movement and stillness. If 51 is the beginning of a cycle, then 52 is the culmination. Like mountains, it stands for accumulation that is not afraid to be seen, and stillness that enables consciousness to expand.

The fact that here we have Mountain upon Mountain indicates that one seeks to be still both outside (the body) and inside (the mind). The practice of yoga is about stillness of the body in the sense that even while carrying out the movements (asanas), one applies awareness. One focuses one's attention successively on all the parts of the body, both those that are active and those that are not, until you are completely relaxed and alive, even in the midst of the pose. With this practice of attention, when it comes time to meditate, one is easily receptive.

Deepak Chopra has written a book about yoga (*Living in the Light*, 2023, with Sarah Platt-Finger), which contains an exercise where you start by focusing on an object in the room, then you soften your gaze and shift your focus to inside your chest. Now you move back and forth between the two points of focus. The exercise, they say, is a way of seeing that your essence is transcendent.

From the I Chng's perspective, this practice evokes 52: Keeping Still: "Keeping his back still so that he no longer feels his body".

In the yoga section of *Living in the Light*, Platt-Finger describes yoga as meaning harness, yoke or unite. She says, "Yoga merges the disparate parts of the self into one unified state of consciousness, allowing us to live fully in the light." With this perception of yoga, it is possible to see what Wilhelm might have meant.

I wondered where Wilhelm's idea came from, however. He wrote his book in the period around 1920. Beyond that, the full text of the I Ching was written around 1100 BC in China, when King Wen expanded the original text and organised it. Wilhelm's statement suggests that yoga (from India) was known in China at that time. Of course, the roots of yoga (in India) go back as far as the I Ching: about 5,000 years. What does this mean for our question?

There are writers who think that the connection of yoga with China goes a long way back. One writer, Deborah Charnes (The Namaste Counsel), says, "In the ancient Mahabharata (Hindu holy writings), there are several references to China, and The Buddha (Siddhartha Gautama) left the Indian subcontinent to settle in China more than 2,000 years ago."

This is not a definitive answer, but it is a suggestion that there was a connection that Wilhelm was alluding to, embracing India and yoga. I take into account that Wilhelm lived in Peking (Beijing) for around two decades, and had a close association with the local I Ching scholars. I am surprised that none of the I Ching commentators whose books I possess followed this thread of thought.

For me, it is natural to follow both yoga and the I Ching. They are amenable compatriots.

54 Following a creed

Richard J. Smith (*The I Ching: A Biography*, 2012) discusses what makes a classic in world literature. He says that a classic must focus on matters of great importance in human life, identifying basic human problems and offering some kind of guidance for dealing with them. It must be beautiful, moving and memorable. And it must be complex, nuanced, comprehensive and profound.

The examples of classics that he gives are the Christian Bible, the Jewish Torah, the Muslim Quran, the Hindu Vedas and the Buddhist sutras, and other writings such as the Odyssey, the Republic, and the Pilgrim's Progress. Smith puts the I Ching in this company, but maintains it is rather different from all of these others.

Structurally, the I Ching lacks any systematic narrative. It is made up, essentially, of sixty-four hexagrams. It offers no vision of spiritual salvation. There is no promise of an afterlife or of reincarnation. There is no Supreme Creator or Deity, or a host of deities. There is no evil presence like Satan.

There are no stories like a great flood or a plague, or the escape of the chosen people from slavery and their journey across the desert to the Promised Land. There is not even a Creation story or an account of the end of the world. So saying, it can be concluded that the I Ching does not offer a creed.

Smith makes the further point that in the scriptures, God reveals only what God chooses to reveal. In China, in contrast, the "mind of Heaven" was available to be known by all, through nature and the I Ching.

It is the movement of yin and yang that explains this different perspective. What is appropriate at one point is movement (51: Thunder), and what is appropriate at another point is stillness (52: Mountain). What is the secret? It was expressed by Lao Tzu in the *Tao Te Ching*: "The Tao that can be told is not the eternal Tao" (in the first chapter).

"Darkness within darkness, the gate to all mystery" (also from the first chapter).

We can observe that Lao Tzu came along (around 500 BC) after the I Ching had been formulated, not before. It expresses what was implicit in the I Ching. For this reason, I think it is futile to try to nail down the "original" version of the I Ching, because the relationship between the I Ching and the culture in which it was birthed was always symbiotic.

I like what John Minford (as one example) has done, in drawing on a multitude of Chinese thinkers from across the centuries in explaining what the lines in the hexagrams mean. The I Ching is a work that needs continual interpretation, from multiple perspectives.

I also bear in mind that my quest is for understanding of life: Heaven, Earth and humanity, rather than a definitive academic treatise or religious catechism. My notes are for the journey.

It is intriguing that the authors of the I Ching did not articulate the ideas that lie beneath it, and develop them into a creed. I have to assume that this omission is deliberate. We may say that the I Ching is accurate in practice, and pertinent, but more than that, it is evocative. It is not a scientific or legal treatise aimed at conquering the world with words and concepts.

It is evocative, with imagery that we must sit with, letting it play in our mind, letting disparate images contend with each other until they find resolution. Moreover, the resolution is more frequently in our heart than in our mind. Some have said that the Chinese saw the heart and mind as one, rather than conceiving of a mind that ruled life in separation from the heart.

Be that as it may. We do not need to have a fixed conception of what the ancient Chinese thought. It is enough that we see that now, we live in a culture that is dominated by the intellect and cleverness. Emotion is seen as messy and weak. I think it is sufficient to reply that this is not a truth; it is an ambit claim. It seems clear enough that if one is to live a full, honest life, one needs to treat the heart and mind as both being essential aspects of our person.

Accordingly, we need to employ the non-verbal aspects of our heart-mind, delving into the imagery the I Ching has given us to see what its truth may be, knowing that this delivers us into the realm of love.

55 Following the true nature

It may seem problematic to say you are not following a creed: "Don't you believe in anything?" But the I Ching's response would be: "We should be steadfast and upright." In living daily life, sometimes we should move, and sometimes we should be still, whether or not we subscribe to a creed. So, we need to seek to understand the true nature of things. Only then will we know when to move and when to be still.

There is a hexagram called Following: 17: Sui.

It is considered to be supreme good fortune. Note, it is in being steadfast that one profits. The hexagram is made up of Thunder below Lake, that is, movement and delight. The hexagram Following calls up the idea that someone follows what is good (delightful). It refers to horses and oxen following a good master, being tamed, and carrying heavy loads over long distances. There has to be resonance between the leader and the follower: I move and others delight.

It also incorporates the idea that people must follow of their own accord; they are not forced. And in a sense, they are not even following the leader; they are always following the true nature of things. If the leader diverges from that, the follower must draw their distance from the leader.

Underlying the concept of Following is the premise that one is operating in freedom from guile. To be steadfast is to be sincere and honest, all the way to one's core. Misfortune is associated with deceit and lies. It is only when one is acting with sincerity that one can do anything of substance. One can have goals and destinations.

To follow is also to be adaptable. This is the essence of the I Ching. Circumstances change, and one must adapt, although retaining one's goals and principles. With sincerity and perseverance, one's capabilities grow. This is what is meant by the saying, "I cultivate my heart and mind."

56 Hindrance

Another day, travelling along in an in-between time. The I Ching says 33: Retreat: Dun. It is a time of smoothness and prosperity. The firm lines are in the right place, and the wise person lives in accord with the will of heaven. It is a time to accept stillness, to confront it. There may also be a need to preserve strength, to recover from trials. The wise person also avoids inferior people, but without wrath.

The third line says: stay at home, care for small things. It is not a time for great endeavours or public ventures. It suggests that there may have been illness, and to be aware that dark forces may still attach.

I appreciate the fact that the I Ching does not paint things all one way. Here it says that the time is prosperous and smooth; one is keeping to oneself and this is appropriate, but then there is a word of caution: there may be illness, and dark forces attached to it. Life is a complete package, and we may not enjoy all of the parts.

The hexagram changes to 12: Hindrance: Pi. There are some hexagrams in the I Ching that you do not want to get. They seem dark and enmeshing. This is one of them. You want to get 11: Peace: Tai. There, everything is just right: Heaven and Earth are in the right relationship to each other, and everything is as it should be. Progress is smooth and unhindered.

33: Retreat: Dun   12: Hindrance: Pi

In 12, it is just the opposite. Heaven and Earth are in the wrong relationship: they are moving away from each other and are not in communication. Nothing goes well and it is the realm of misfortune. But, we need to remind ourselves that the I Ching contains all the possible situations in life, and this is one of them.

Also, the occurrence of this combination of Heaven and Earth is not avoidable. When things proceed to their limit, they alternate to their reverse. It is part of the flow of things. It is unfavourable even for the superior person. The great departs and the little arrives.

What do superior persons do in this situation? They restrain themselves and they continue in virtue in order to avoid calamity. And they do not seek to blame others. They do not grasp at high position or for honours and rewards. They live modestly.

Importantly, the superior person acknowledges that danger is present. They do not ignore it or neglect it. They make sure that they do not become self-satisfied, a condition which attracts misfortune.

Huang mentions death. The superior person is always aware of death, even when times are good, in fact, especially when times are good. Because we are mortal; that is the condition of our existence. We rise and we fall; we arrive and we depart. So it will ever be.

12 is a hard circumstance, but we need to examine it directly. We need to see it in the context of the whole of reality. We are at a certain point in space and time. It is not a favourable point, but neither is it a fixed point. Change continues to occur. But we need to know how to live at this point, to see it in the context of the whole. When we can embrace it wholeheartedly, we can move on.

So, I am reminded of death, and danger. Yet, the appropriate response is that of the poet that John Minford quotes: Xie Lingyun (385-433 AD): "I cultivate my heart and mind. I live at leisure."

57 Old paths, new paths

When we say "old paths", we may be thinking of twenty or more years ago: the earlier years of our own lives. We may be thinking of one or two hundred years ago: a time in our society before our own time. Perhaps there were horses and carriages. Or we may be thinking of a long time ago: a distant time, before current nations and preoccupations.

When we say "old paths", we may be thinking of relevance. Do people need to tread there anymore? It may be nostalgic, but it is not relevant to our current environment. To be tough about it, it is just escapism. But Cary Baynes (the translator of Richard Wilhelm's version of the I Ching) talked about the I Ching as being about the "continent of the spirit", our "inner space", which is ever-relevant. We need to understand ourselves and our psyche as much as ever we did. Baynes called it "the ultimate human goal".

Even in the span of one lifetime, old paths can become overgrown or smudged out. In our society, for many people there is no alternative perspective to the daily news and social media. There is no point of view expressed that does not have a business outcome in mind. The result of this environment is that if a view about human values is ever expressed, it is generally sentimental.

The forces for money, unemotional objectivity and superficial social status are ubiquitous and relentless.

As an academic pursuit the I Ching is not dead, but as a living companion for self-examination and self-development, is it down to one old book in a big-city bookshop?

The I Ching is an old path, one of the oldest on the planet. It has always been a book of great esteem in Chinese culture. Over the centuries it filtered through other Asian countries: Korea, Japan, Vietnam (Richard Smith, 2012) and became part of their cultures. In recent centuries it found its way into Western countries. But has all such exploration been swamped by technology and Western triumphalism?

In Zen Buddhism, the river is always new. If we sit there and watch it, the water that flows past us is not the same as a moment before. And nor are we the same person. This points us to the inner world. In the inner sense, this is something more than a trite saying. And the new path only makes sense when one has given up wanting to bring the world to order.

"The Tao that can be told is not the eternal Tao."

The old path is not the old path. I continue.

The I Ching says 22: Adornment: Bi. It changes to 20: Watching/Tower: Guan.

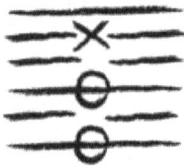

22: Adorning: Bi   20: Watching: Guan

In Adornment, a Fire is at the foot of the Mountain. Imagine the light being cast up the slopes of the mountain at night, a gorgeous scene. When do we find Adornment? It is when a society has stabilised and violence is minimal, so that wealth can accumulate. Then it is possible for people to care about the look of things.

One commentator, Deng Ming-Dao, makes the comment: "Adornment integrates the wearer with the spirit world." The beauty of adornment evokes the ideas of beauty and perfection. It is a suggestion of something more, something higher than the ordinary and the difficult times of life. With it we can express the highest hopes of ourselves and our society.

At the same time, the I Ching reminds us that adornment is only on the surface. It is the quality of the spirit within that is essential. In the stages of things, there is a beginning, there is growth, there are trials, there are defeats and victories, and there is the expression of joy. Along with it, there is the articulation of the principles that we strive to be true to.

Adornment is not the province of the wealthy only. It is the province of those who align with upright values and wish to express the beauty of those principles. The core is everlasting and upright.

We understand adornment as a manifestation of the state of a society, but it may be likewise a manifestation of individual grace. When one's inner state is calm, stable and wisely directed, it becomes visible. The Fire throws its light up the Mountain.

In consideration of old paths, the I Ching asks us to consider what is inherently beautiful. It is not merely external beauty that distracts us from an empty life; it is beauty that is true to the core. It is not ephemeral, like the shiny new things that do not last. It is beauty that is alive in the midst of life.

The I Ching then switches to 20: Watching: Guan. The image is of a Tower. In China, there were memorial gates, built on high vantage points and visible from afar, which were both places from which to see and places from which one could be seen. Sacrifices were made there. The important thing was the sincerity of the person making the sacrifice.

When we are watching life, life is also watching us. What we see is affected by where we stand and what our perspective is, our attitude. The life that the I Ching is commending to us is of awareness and self-examination. Gradually, says Hua-Ching Ni, one becomes unaffected by the pressures of worldly life and stays attuned to the deepest levels of our nature. To be swayed by the concerns of the world is to become lost.

The story here is of the ancient kings who inspected their regions and established the right teachings for the people. The king set a good example and corrected himself continually. He encouraged moral responsibility. He took time to let everything come into view. He confronted his faults and worked to eliminate them.

The Wind works through subtle penetration, blowing across the Earth, the receptive. Beginning with the subjective (who am I? what do I see?), we come to realise that we are also seen by others (what is the example? where is the spirit?).

The I Ching commends to us a life of seeing deeply, letting everything come into view and considering it calmly, from a position of reverence and virtue.

Of this reading, it can also be said that the I Ching is speaking of itself. It is the adornment to our lives and it is the tower of watching and seeing.

Just so, we continue.

58 Epilogue 1

I thought I had finished. However, I thought I should ask the I Ching if I had finished. So I asked, is there more to be said in the book?

The answers were teasing: 64: Before Completion (Not Yet Fulfilled): Wei Ji, changing to 4: Youthful Folly (Childhood): Meng.

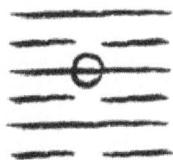

64: Not Yet Fulfilled: Wei Ji   4: Childhood: Meng

In what way teasing? Hexagram 64 seemed to suggest that I had not finished. The trigrams are Water and Fire, and here, Fire is above Water: not in their correct positions. I remember, when Water is above Fire, you can boil the kettle and make a cup of tea. That is the image of perfection, or completion. Therefore, when the configuration is not correct, one has to continue.

But, in 4: Youthful Folly, there is a youth who asks a question, and after they get an answer, they ask the same question again, just like the child who keeps asking "why?". This time, the teacher refuses to answer; the youth is being importunate. I think, asking the I Ching whether I have finished the book or not is like the youth who keeps asking the same question. The reality is, there is nothing further to be said.

Accordingly, I can go back to the first hexagram I got and say, when one thinks one is at the end, it is appropriate to ask oneself if one is

189

at the end. However, the answer may be that there is nothing more to be said; one is indeed at the end.

There was one moving line in the first hexagram, the fourth. It said: "Perseverance will bring good fortune. The general subjugates the land after three years. Regret vanishes." In terms of the book, if I were a general, I could say that the land has been subjugated. The "three years" suggests that I have spent sufficient effort in addressing all the aspects I thought I should address. I should not try to push it further than is appropriate.

59 Epilogue 2

However, I wonder if there is something more to be said about my medical episode. Have I directly asked the I Ching whether the subject of this book contributed to the stroke? No, and I should do that. This is the time to do it.

I threw the coins and obtained a hexagram with no moving lines. This means that the commentary that I will consult is Richard Rudd's book on Gene Keys.

The hexagram was 23: Splitting Apart: Bo. Rudd calls it "The Alchemy of Simplicity".

The three stages of this gene key are Complexity, Simplicity and Quintessence. Complexity is the Shadow; Simplicity is the Gift, and Quintessence is the Siddhi.

As ever, Rudd takes me on a long journey. Immediately, even before I start reading, I think of myself in terms of splitting apart. This would be one way of describing what happened to me in early November. Rudd would be suggesting that in a state of complexity I experienced a crisis. The aftermath was a process of simplifying, and the discovery of Quintessence, the essence of things.

Rudd is much bolder than I am. Nevertheless, I decide to go on the journey, and see what he has to say.

Rudd's account starts with a discussion of words. Language is one result of our efforts to control our environment. The problem is that because we live in the shadow of fears, our words invariably serve to make things more complex, rather than simpler and clearer. So, for a start, we could say that our words split the world apart rather than bringing it together.

Part of the reason for this complication of things is that we are deaf to others as well as to ourselves. This deafness is, again, the result of our fears. We may fear not being accepted, so we strive to be liked or to be authoritative. Often, however, our efforts to communicate result in misunderstandings and anger. And that contributes to ongoing difficulties in expressing ourselves.

The better path is to speak (or write) simply, avoiding clutter, jargon and complication in our communications. Rudd expresses this in terms of a gift, when fears are let go. We can then be direct, precise and concise. There is no waste in what we say. It slows things down, and lessens the need to say everything, or to say it perfectly. There is a trust that things will resolve themselves in their own time.

So far, I can go with Rudd's distinctions. I strive for simplicity, not complication, in what I write. I am not trying to dazzle or confuse the reader. I would hope that what I have said about the I Ching makes sense and makes it inviting. On the other hand, I don't deny that I had reservations about this project and wondered if it would crash in transit. And after the big headache, I thought that I needed to get in control.

Rudd says this: "Splitting Apart", beyond the gift of Simplicity, is about opening up our centre to our quintessence. It splits us apart from our fears and illusions. "Your thoughts are split apart. Your entire body may undergo a period of profound physical sensation, and the continuity of your thinking is destroyed. What remains afterwards is consciousness itself speaking through the shell of your personality."

This, he says, is completely outside of your control. You cannot master it as a technique. One path is logic and technology. The second path is emotion (the way of the poet, the artist and the musician). But the middle way is to accept the mystery of what happens. One goes through a complete deconstruction and you are left in the present, conscious and alive.

Rudd urges us to trust our own inner path, and not to expect it to follow convention: "It is a path sculpted from the void."

It leaves me with the question: what if what happened in early November was not an unforeseen disaster, but a doorway? And to put up that question, I have to know that there can be no confirmation from any external authority. It would be my conclusion that I choose to live with.

This leads to more questions. What if I did exactly the right thing by keeping my gaze on this book, and continuing to write, after the headache, insofar as I could, day by day? During this period, I told no one what I was doing. Nor was I trying to be doggedly persistent; I simply wanted to continue trying to express my conception of the I Ching from my unique experience. My thoughts were indeed split apart for a while. For a time, I did think that my thinking had been destroyed.

Now, I have followed the thread of the book through to its natural end, accompanied by the I Ching itself.

I am glad to have ended up with the concept of Quintessence, the essence and spirit of things. It seems appropriate. The *Shorter Oxford English Dictionary* defines it (one of its several definitions) as the most essential part of any substance. Its meaning, fittingly, goes back to the concept of the "fifth essence" of ancient and medieval philosophy, thought to be the substance of which the heavenly bodies were composed, and to be actually latent in all things.

Just so, we continue.

60 Epilogue 3

There should be an epilogue for the I Ching itself. I started with the apparent loss of the I Ching from sight in our current society. I have maintained that this would be a great loss to the world. I have tried to show its value in my own life over a long period of time: in fact, for most of my life.

I say we should return to the well of goodness, the I Ching. Brian Browne Walker (1993) describes it as a source of spiritual nourishment. In fact, he says, we need two wells! One is for external guidance in our involvement in the affairs of the world. The other is for internal guidance, to cultivate our own good character. In both cases, the goal is our continual development.

The I Ching is inexhaustible. In accessing it we need to develop a practice that is like accessing a well: the rope must be strong, and long enough, the bucket must be intact, and handled with care so that it is not broken, the sides of the well must be kept in order, and the water should not be muddied. And one must drink the water; wisdom must be put into practice.

One more thing: we should acknowledge the clear water deep inside ourselves, and deep inside others.

Thus will we meet with success.

Appendix 1: Moving lines

When the three coins are used, they are thrown six times. One side of the coin is denoted 2 (yin) and the other side is 3 (yang). This means that the possible outcomes are 6, 7, 8 and 9.

The lines are drawn horizontally, one on top of the other, beginning with the first line at the bottom. There are four types of lines, based on the four possible outcomes:

- 6: yin (female) – a broken line which is a moving line
- 7: yang (male) – an unbroken line
- 8: yin – a broken line
- 9: yang – an unbroken line which is a moving line.

The first hexagram is determined by ignoring the fact that the moving lines are moving. That is, 6 is read as yin and 9 is read as yang. The hexagram is made up of a lower trigram (the bottom three lines) and an upper trigram (the top three lines). Most I Ching books contain a table (a Key) which displays the upper and lower trigrams, and this enables you to find the resulting hexagram (1 to 64).

The judgement and commentary on the hexagram are then read. If there are any moving lines, then the commentary on those moving lines is read also. The moving lines indicate how the situation is evolving.

——✕——	6	Yin, Feminine	Moving line
————	7	Yang, Masculine	Unmoving line
—— ——	8	Yin, Feminine	Unmoving line
——o——	9	Yang, Masculine	Moving line

If there are any moving lines, each moving line is now transposed into its opposite – the moving yin line becomes yang, and the moving yang line becomes yin. A new hexagram is then obtained, and the table is consulted again to find the new hexagram. The judgement for this hexagram is read (and the text for the individual lines is ignored). The second hexagram indicates what the situation is evolving towards.

| ——⊖—— | Moving yang changes to yin | ▬▬ ▬▬ |
| ——✕—— | Moving yin changes to yang | ——————— |

Bibliography

I Ching books

-----, 1971, I Ching Cards, Agmuller, Switzerland.

Carol K. Anthony, 1981, *The Philosophy of the I Ching*, Anthony Publishing, Stow MA.

Carol Anthony, 1988, *A Guide to the I Ching*, 3rd ed., Anthony Publishing, Stow MA.

John Blofeld, 1968, *I Ching: The book of change*, Dutton, New York.

Chan Chiu Ming, 1997, *Book of Changes: An interpretation for the modern age*, Asiapac, Singapore.

Thomas Cleary, 1986, *The Taoist I Ching*, Shambhala, Boston MA.

Deng Ming-Dao, 2006, *The Living I Ching: Using ancient Chinese wisdom to shape your life*, Harper One, New York.

Khigh Alx Dhiegh, 1973, *The Eleventh Wing: An exposition of the dynamics of I Ching for now*, Delta, New York.

Michael Graeme, 2007, *The Hexagrams of the Book of Changes*, Rivendale Review, England.

Roger Green, 2004, *The I Ching Workbook*, New Holland, Sydney.

Diana ffarington Hook,1973, *The I Ching and You*, Routledge, London.

Hua-Ching Ni, 1983, *I Ching: The book of changes and the unchanging truth*, Seven Star Communications, Santa Monica, CA.

Alfred Huang, 1998, *The Complete I Ching*, Inner Traditions International, Rochester VT.

Neyma Jahan, 2012, *The Celestial Dragon I Ching*, Watkins, London.

Stephen Karcher, 2003, *Total I Ching: Myths for change*, Time Warner, London.

Stephen Karcher, 2009, *I Ching: The symbolic life*, Booksurge.

Lao Tzu, 1972, *Tao Te Ching*, trans. Gia-Fu Feng and Jane English, Vintage, New York.

James Legge, 1964 (1882), *I Ching: Book of changes*, University Books, Secaucus NJ.

Richard John Lynn, 1994, *The Classic of Changes*, Columbia University Press, New York.

Gary Melyan and Wen-Kuang Chu, 2003, *I Ching: The perfect companion*, Black Dog & Leventhal, New York.

John Minford, 2014, *I Ching (Yiching): The book of change*, Viking, New York.

Joseph Murphy, *Secrets of the I Ching*, 2000, Prentice Hall, New York.

Neil Powell, 1979, *The Book of Change*, Orbis, London.

Geoffrey Redmond, 2017, *The I Ching (Book of Changes): A critical translation of the ancient text*, Bloomsbury, London.

Nigel Richmond, 1985, *The I Ching Oracle*, privately published, pdf.

Richard Rudd, 2009, *Gene Keys: Unlocking the higher purpose in your DNA*, Watkins, London.

Mondo Secter, 1993, *The I Ching Handbook: Decision-making with and without divination*, North Atlantic Books, Berkley CA.

W.A. Sherrill and W.K. Chu, 1989, *An Anthology of I Ching*, Arkana, London.

Richard J. Smith, 2012, *The I Ching: A biography*, Princeton University Press, Princeton NJ.

Brian Browne Walker, 1993, *The I Ching or Book of Changes*, Piatkus, London.

Richard Wilhelm, 1975 (1950), *The I Ching or Book of Changes*, trans. by Richard Wilhelm into German, rendered into English by Cary Baynes, Routledge & Kegan Paul, London.

Richard Wilhelm, 1962 (1931), *The Secret of the Golden Flower*, trans. Cary Baynes, Harvest/HBJ, New York.

R.L. Wing, 1979, *The I Ching Workbook*, Harmony Books, New York.

Wu Wei, 2005, *The I Ching: The book of answers*, Power Press, Los Angeles CA.

Other books

Rita Carter, 1998, *Mapping the Mind,* Weidenfeld and Nicolson, London.

Timothy Chappell, 2009, *Ethics and Experience*, McGill-Queen's University Press, Montreal.

Deepak Chopra and Sarah Platt-Finger, 2023, *Living in the Light*, Rider, London.

Norman Doidge, 2015, *The Brain's Way of Healing,* Scribe, Brunswick, Victoria.

Robert Greenleaf, 1977, *Servant Leadership,* Paulist Press, Mahwah NJ.

John Haught, 2017, *The New Cosmic Story*, Yale University Press, London.

Robert Hopcke, 1997, *There Are No Accidents,* Penguin.

Joseph Jaworski, 2011, *Synchronicity: The inner path of leadership,* Berrett-Koehler, San Francisco CA.

Carl Jung, 1985 (1952), *Synchronicity: An acausal connecting principle,* Routledge.

Iain McGilchrist, 2019, *The Master and His Emissary: The divided brain and the making of the western world*, Yale University Press, London.

David Roland, 2014, *How I Rescued My Brain,* Scribe, Brunswick, Victoria.

Margrit Segesman, 1973, *Wings of Power: Progressive yoga relaxation*, Hill of Content, Melbourne.

Peter Senge, 1990, *The Fifth Discipline: The art and practice of the learning organization*, Random House, Sydney.

Yanis Varoufakis, 2024, *Technofeudalism*, Vintage, London.

Acknowledgments

Thank you to friends and family who expressed concern about my health and offered support during the period after the episode of the big headache.

Thank you also to the early readers who spent time with the draft copy and offered me sage advice, especially Nikki Thompson and Marion Sinclair.

Note, there are some things that this book does not contain, such as a key for finding the hexagram(s) once you have established the two trigrams and converted any moving lines. My reasoning is that this book is neither a translation nor a commentary on the I Ching. It is best to obtain an I Ching book and have it with you, in the same way that you read a travel guide with a map alongside you.

Author profile

Glenn Martin is the author of over twenty-five books. He is an independent scholar, researcher and writer. He has written on ethics and values, family history, reflections on experience, and he has produced several volumes of poetry. His scattered career includes teaching in high schools and at tertiary level, management of community-sector organisations, writing commentary on employment law and management for professional publications, editing a national magazine for trainers, and designing online education courses. He has graduated from the workforce.

Glenn lives in Sydney. He has also lived in the hills in far northern New South Wales, where he wrote two books of local history. He has five children and four grandchildren.

This is Glenn's first book that is focused on the I Ching; he has used it for personal reflection for fifty years. Previously he had written one novel (a reflection on experience) where the I Ching was mentioned: *The Ten Thousand Things* (2010).

Other books by Glenn Martin

Stories/Reflections on experience

The Ten Thousand Things (2010)
Sustenance (2011)
To the Bush and Back to Business (2012)
The Big Story Falls Apart (2014)
The Quilt Approach: A Tasmanian Patchwork (2020)
Long Time Approaching: An Incomplete Memoir (2023)
Travel with a Pen (2023)
Library Meets Book Fair (2024)

Books on ethics and values

Human Values and Ethics in the Workplace (2010)
The Little Book of Ethics: A Human Values Approach (2011)
The Concise Book of Ethics (2012)
A Foundation for Living Ethically (2020)
Future: The Spiritual Story of Humanity (2020)

Books on family history

A Modest Quest (2017)
The Search for Edward Lewis (2018)
They Went to Australia (2019)
No Gold in Melbourne: A Scottish Family in Australia (2021)
All the Rivers Come Together: Tracing Family (2022)

The Sailor, the Baron and the Dressmaker (2024)

Poetry collections

Flames in the Open (2007)
Love and Armour (2007)
Volume 4: I in the Stream (2017)
Volume 3: That Was Then: The Early Poems Project (2019)
The Way Is Open (2020)

Local history

Places in the Bush: A History of Kyogle Shire (1988)
The Kyogle Public School Centenary Book (1995)

www.ingramcontent.com/pod-product-compliance
Lightning Source LLC
Chambersburg PA
CBHW052040090426
42739CB00010B/1982